CW01666183

BURN IDENTITY

by

Christopher Burn

First published in 2021

by DHH Publishing

The Old Joiners Shop

Skirling by Biggar, ML12 6HD

Scotland, UK

A CIP record for this book is available from the British Library

ISBN 978-1-9996691-0-2

for Margie, without whom much of this did not happen
and
for Alfie, Ben, Olivia, Oscar, Sophie, for whom much will happen

——)(——

FOREWORD - FAMILY MATTERS

Camberley, in Surrey is a quiet, respectable and very English town, even in 1942, in the middle of World War II. It is very different from noisy, chaotic Bombay, India. A child of two can see that. And that child is me.

The house of Lieutenant-Colonel the Hon. Bertrand Joseph Russell, DSO, is called Silverwood. It is on the quieter side of Camberley, and it's warm and spacious, but who are all these people? And who is Colonel Russell? And why are there so many dogs (at least a dozen) jumping up and licking my face? and most of all, who is this lady called Auntie Prue who says she's going to be my new mother?

My sisters Lucinda and Caroline sit beside me on a sort of bench in the hallway and I can tell they are uneasy too, but at least they are older than me and therefore, must know more. I shall have to ask them as soon as possible.

These are all part of my earliest memories. Our arrival seems like the end of a very long journey, but there are suddenly lots of new questions to be answered too. It is all very confusing.

Yet, the big house feels immediately warm and welcoming on this strange early autumn afternoon. And after the journey that we have been on, we need a place to rest.

Our wartime trek, half-way round the world, fleeing from the Japanese armies and later from German air and sea forces, covered thousands of miles. It began with our escape from Hong Kong where my father, a British Army major had died, shortly before its capture by Japanese forces. From there, on the last plane to escape, our small group of my mother and her three youngest children plus her good friend Rachel, reached Rangoon in southern Burma. But little time could be taken for rest there, as the marauding Japanese approached. So, we took the long road North through Burma (mainly by bus or on foot) into India where relative safety lay, though the hardship in getting there was immense. Later, by troop ship, in convoy pursued by German U-boats, we made an arduous sea journey round the Cape, back eventually to England. To my grandfather's house in Camberley, at teatime.

Much of this trip was highly dangerous, it was always stressful, and very, very tiring. Such indeed were the demands it made on our poor mother that by the time we had reached India in early 1942, she was utterly exhausted. Unable to continue, she collapsed and died shortly after arrival, of a brain haemorrhage, brought on by extreme over-exertion.

These images are the starting point of my story. As I summon them up now, they bring back many feelings, most of which would remain through my childhood and beyond – feelings of loss, grief and anxiety.

It was an important moment for me when I finally decided that I was not going to remain a sponge, forever soaked in these events and feelings: instead, I was going to be defined by my response.

God works through other people, they say. We should give God a try. He sends helpers. I have been blessed because I was sent a lot of helpers, not least my wife Margie and my children Alex, Johnnie and Annabel.

Life changes from fairy story to horror story, from tragedy to farce and from reality to magic. It isn't a box of chocolates – it's a box of fireworks. And everybody gets one.

The family we find ourselves born into results from pure chance, but is hugely important. Our family shapes who we are, more than anything else. Family matters.

While my family struggled with travel and disruption in far off lands, Margie's family struggled in Colchester, Essex with food shortages, sirens and the sound of the Luftwaffe overhead. We were both war babies with stories to tell.

Margie is not able to tell her side. I have tried in various chapters to recount her story, but my poor attempt is less entertaining than her own words would be. I wish it were otherwise.

What has happened in both our lifetimes (so far) is set out in the chapters of Part One. There is also a Part Two, which deals with ancestry and which contains some surprising facts.

I hope that nothing I have said will offend. My intention has been to give the truth and not to upset anyone. Indeed, rather than crying havoc, I fear I have let slip the dogs of boredom.

It's natural to want to know about one's ancestors, both recent and distant. I hope that writing this account, many years afterwards, will shed a truthful light on what happened and on what has followed in the years since - the good and the bad. For time is the great healer. And truth, they say, is the daughter of time.

PRELUDE

It is 1921 - the decade of the Roaring Twenties. Four teenagers are growing up, in the way teenagers do, in different and distant parts of the world. At this pivotal time, a hundred years ago, they are excited but also anxious.

The Great War of 1914-18 and the influenza pandemic that follows it (both as bad in terms of loss of life as anything seen recently), are raw and very fresh memories. The world seems full of dread and disorder but it also feels new and stimulating. They are not dismayed - they dream of great things to come.

Here are our hopeful four:

Mary Stuart – aged 14, in Picton, New Zealand.
Ronnie Reid – aged 15, in Salisbury, England
Ursula Russell – aged 16, in London, England
Stanford Burn – aged 17, in Durban, South Africa.

Destiny or chance? Unconnected and widely distanced, they will meet, as two separate couples, and marry. Both weddings take place in England, in the same year - 1929.

What random events, what timing brings these young people together? It is impossible to say. When you look at genetics through the lens of chaos theory, you'll probably wish you hadn't. The possibilities are limitless.

Yet, romantic chemistry happens for each of these couples. Exactly how, when or where Stanford first meets Ursula, and Ronnie first meets Mary, we do not know. But It happens, and their first encounters progress eventually to marriage and families.

Between them, they will be responsible for a total of nine children, numerous grand-children and a spectacular number of great-grand-children. What's more, they will brew up a pretty good mix of genes for future generations.

Yet, they cannot foresee how relatively short their married lives together will be.

Today, those four teenagers lie buried far from each other, in four different countries – England, Scotland, India and Hong Kong, their worldly tasks done.

Every life contains highs and lows, successes and failures. These lives were no different from many others. Each of the four experienced great emotional pain as well as moments of great joy, as most people do.

Mary, Ronnie, Ursula and Stanford were all fine people who achieved many things and deserve to be remembered, and I for one, am particularly grateful to them, because they were the respective parents of Margie and myself. Both born in 1940, we met and started a new branch of the Burn family.

Young people today probably feel the same as our four teenagers did in 1920. The challenges are different, but not that different. To them I say: trust in God, do what's right and always hope for the best, but plan for the unexpected. Whatever happens is likely to surprise you.

PART ONE – FAMILY LIFE

Chapter 1

The Gin Drinkers Line – Panic In Hong Kong

The Assyrian came down like the wolf on the fold,
And his cohorts were gleaming in purple and gold (Byron)

The Hong Kong Telegraph did not record my birth on the twenty-first of October 1940. Much more surprisingly, since World War II had been going extremely badly for over a year, the paper on that day seemed untroubled by thoughts of any threat to Hong Kong itself. It appeared to have seen the British colony as safely removed from the terrible fighting in Europe.

Yet little more than twelve months later, on December the seventh, 1941 - the same day as Pearl Harbour was attacked, Japanese air strikes were made on Hong Kong and Singapore. One can only imagine the sense of panic that must have gripped the colony, following these onslaughts. The surprise campaign on the inadequately garrisoned island did not take long. Hong Kong fell to the Japs on Christmas Day 1941.

Churchill's government had apparently decided early in the war, that Hong Kong was too small and too distant to be worth fighting hard for.

The Hong Kong defences relied heavily on the oddly-named Gin Drinkers Line. This was a British military defensive line on the Hong Kong mainland, built to the same concept and roughly at the same time as France's Maginot Line, built after World War I. The British believed the line could protect the colony from Japanese invasion for at least six months and even called it the "Oriental Maginot Line". Unfortunately, the Gin Drinkers Line proved even more ineffective than its French equivalent.

The Hongkong Telegraph.

FIRST EDITION

MONDAY, OCTOBER 21, 1940

Spectacular Show By British Airmen

TERRIFIC ATTACK ON FRENCH PORTS

PREMIER SAW IT SHOT DOWN

Air Action In Mediterranean Intensifies

R.A.F. HAMMER AT ITALIAN BASES

Burma Rd. Bombing Resumed

Latest Japanese Claims

Political Alignment With Axis Is Denied

GERMAN PLANES THWARTED

Fail To Reach London

CHEERFUL MR. CHURCHILL

TAKE THE LIMELIGHT

Turkey, Bulgaria And Greece

CHANNEL GUN DUEL

The War's Biggest Bombardment

Pres. Taft As An Evacuee Ship

Britain May Accept Russia's Conquests

Latest London Theories

Peace Commission Plane Crashes

LATEST

Jews Want To Battle Alongside Britons

NAZIS DENY NEW PENETRATIONS

Germans Surprised At England's Resistance

Special to the "Telegraph"

Hong Kong Telegraph 21.10.1940

The Japanese generals also believed the line would stop their advance, until their scouts found out the line was very weak. The Hong Kong garrison simply didn't have anything like enough manpower to do the job expected of it. The Gin Drinkers Line is now considered to have been a complete failure. The line and the whole of Kowloon were abandoned by the British troops in just two days. There can be said to be three main reasons:

- Insufficient troops: although their weaponry was sound, there were not enough British soldiers to maximise the Line's potential. For example, the large Shing Mun Redoubt should have garrisoned over 120 men but was manned by just 30.
- Insufficient training: most of the Hong Kong Garrison was composed of new recruits lacking field experience and proper training.
- Underestimation of the Japanese: the British assumed that the Japanese did not wage night battles and relaxed their guard. They were also overconfident of the Line's capabilities and believed that the Japanese could be easily repulsed.

How wrong they were. The comparatively easy Japanese victory and the British surrender were followed by atrocities on the island and imprisonment in dire conditions for British subjects.

Shortly before the colony's surrender, Major Stanford Burn, of the second battalion The Royal Scots, a part of the meagre British Army garrison on the island, died from gunshot wounds - he may have shot himself. He was my father. His actions are still unclear. He was aged 37 and reports of his death are hard to follow. It appears that in the desperate final days of the defence of Hong Kong, he had difficulty deploying the men under his command who appeared reluctant to follow his orders. Some accounts state the possibility that he was shot by his own men. It was certainly a bad situation, perhaps made worse by panic. In the desperate position they found themselves in, my father's regiment, the Royal Scots, were thought by some to have given up the fight too readily. This view is shown in at least one published account of the battle:

"..a number of derogatory reports and rumours circulated about their (the Royal Scots) performance. One was that the battalion second-in-command, Major Stanford Burn, who had gone forward to try to sort out the mess, was shot by his own men. A more charitable version was that he shot himself when he realised he could do nothing to stop the rot. It is certainly true that for long afterwards the Royal Scots who pride themselves on being the 'First of Foot' were known by many as the 'Fleet of Foot'. In fairness it must be said that they did much to redeem their reputation on the island." From 'Prisoner of the Turnip Heads: Horror, Hunger and Humour in Hong Kong 1941-1945' By G Wright-Nooth, 1994.
We will probably never know the true story of Stanford's death. It is perhaps significant that after the war, the Royal Scots were refused the right to name

Hong Kong among their battle honours, despite making a formal request.

In the book 'Not the Slightest Chance' by Tony Banham, it is noted: "A wartime rumour said that Major Burn had been shot by his own men during the Kowloon fighting... I surmise that it was a feeling of disgrace that he was unable to prevent his battalion breaking up near the pencil factory on December the eleventh, which caused the late Major Burn to take his own life....He was sent there to attempt to restore order, thus death at his own hand following failure seems credible."

Major Stanford Burn, 1940

Stanford lies buried in the British Military Cemetery at Hong Kong. I like to think that he tried his best, in a very desperate situation that could not be controlled. In the official war records his death is listed as "killed in action". His distraught wife Ursula, my mother, had left with three of her children, a few days earlier. Her oldest child, Jancis was already safely in the UK, where she attended boarding school.

What a disastrous time it was for all of us. The fall of Hong Kong and other British outposts in the far East was a chaotic time and marked a low point in World War II. And worse was to come. Mercifully, I remember nothing of this in any detail.

Chapter 2

Unhappy Highways - A Long Walk Through Burma

Does the road wind uphill all the way?
Yes, to the very end (Rossetti)

After escaping from Hong Kong to Burma, Ursula wondered what to do next. With her children and her great friend Rachel Harland, whose husband, Hector was also a British army officer in Hong Kong, they were staying at Moulmein, south of Rangoon, in a large house called Hopeville.

Here is a poignant letter she sent from Burma about this time, to my eldest sister Jancis (then aged 11) in boarding school at Mayfield Convent, in England. You can tell that Ursula has not yet heard of the fall of Hong Kong as she talks of returning there. News travelled slowly in those days.

Hopeville
Moulmein, Burma

Darling Jancis,
Thank you so much for your letter which I was so pleased to get. It was the first one from you and has taken three months to get here. I was so glad to get the snapshot of yourself and Fay having a picnic. I thought it was very good and you have certainly grown a lot. Do send me some more photos of yourself if you ever have any.
Here are some snapshots of all of us. Have not Lucinda and Caroline grown big? And don't you think Christopher is rather sweet? He is growing up very fast, and tries hard to talk, though he only succeeds in making the tiniest little

talking noises.

I am also enclosing a picture of this house. It is really rather nice and has a very nice big garden. I don't know at all how long we are likely to remain here. I wish they would let us go back to Hong Kong, if we can't get back to England. I am glad that all is well with you. I wonder if Mayfield gets a lot of air raids.

Goodbye darling, and lots of love and kisses from us all, Mummy.

As the war continued and the bad news got worse, Ursula must have decided to undertake the difficult journey to India. By then, she probably had little choice.

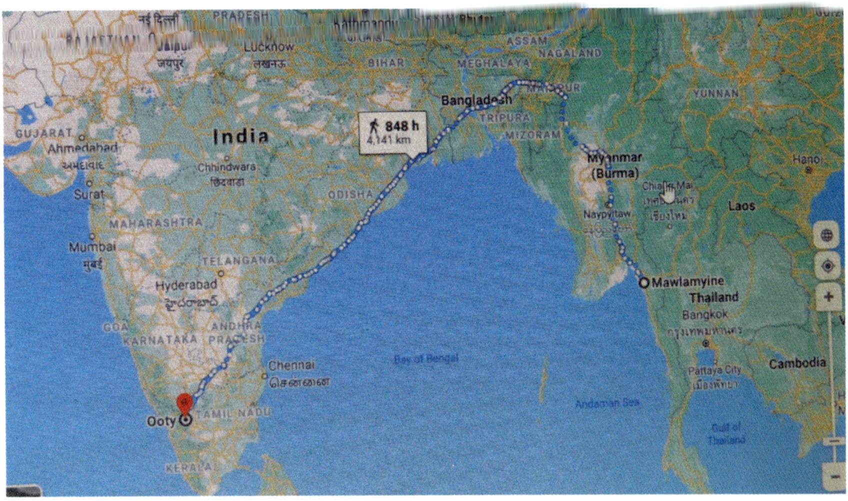

Journey Moulmein to Ooty, 1942

From Moulmein in Burma to the border country with the Indian subcontinent at Kohima, is a distance of many hundreds of miles. It is still a dangerous and difficult journey today. For a mother and three small children in 1941, it must have been appalling, even with the assistance of her faithful friend, Rachel.

But we were not by any means alone in trying – most of the expats in Burma at the time were following the same route, desperately trying to escape before the Japanese armies overtook them and either killed them or perhaps worse, took them prisoner. This exodus is a historical event that is not well known, because it was just one of so many at that time.

"Japan's invasion of Burma prompted many from Burma's Indian, Anglo-Indian and British communities to flee to the safety of India. While some, particularly wealthier people, were able to leave by air or sea, hundreds of thousands were forced to make their way on foot across Burma's mountainous border with India. Thousands died along the way from disease, exhaustion, malnutrition, or through drowning while trying to cross Burma's many rivers.

The retreat was conducted in horrible circumstances. Starving refugees, disorganised stragglers, and the sick and wounded clogged the primitive roads and tracks leading to India.

At least 500,000 civilian fugitives reached India, while an unknown number, conservatively estimated between 10,000 and 50,000, died along the way. In later months, 70 to 80% of those who reached India were afflicted with diseases such as dysentery, smallpox, malaria or cholera, with 30% "desperately so" (Wikipedia – Japanese conquest of Burma)

My memory contains almost no images of this traumatic journey, but I do have one very strange recollection: we are hiding in a ditch and being told to stay very quiet – in front of us is rising ground and beyond the rise there is something very bad, I don't know what. I just hear a strange thumping noise that gets gradually louder. We are all very frightened .... Whatever this was, for some years afterwards the same horrible feeling would sometimes wake me in the middle of the night. My sisters told me they would also have nightmares about this journey.

British novelist H E Bates wrote a fictionalised story of a similar trip through Burma which is said to be an accurate portrayal of the experience. It is called The Jacaranda Tree and I must say I found it an evocative though rather depressing read:

Bates's second novel of the Far East depicts the escape to India of various residents of a Burmese village. Bates notes that while "I had seen the terrain and the people and had absorbed the electrifying atmosphere of central Burma through not only my eyes but the very pores of my skin, I had seen not one inch of the far distant territory over which the long and tragic trek to India had been made in bitter and horrifying circumstances when the Japanese had occupied Singapore and invaded Burma in 1942." He proudly relates a conversation with a survivor of that retreat who found his description completely accurate, as evidence of the success of his "imagination and instinct." some details of the book were "derived from a diary Bates purchased from one who survived the retreat (from the HE Bates Companion).

Having at last reached India, our little party, with assistance from the locals, struggled on for another thousand miles, until they reached the haven of Ootacamund in Southern India. This idyllic spot was a great favourite in peacetime among British expats and was affectionately known as Ooty. Here, we were given a real welcome and the prospect of respite from our exertions. Sadly, this was not to be.

Chapter 3

Disaster In Ooty – The Death Of Ursula

And though I was a soul in pain
My pain I could not feel (Wilde)

Our hopes of a peaceful time were soon cruelly interrupted by the tragic death of Ursula who never recovered from the physical, mental and emotional damage of the previous few months. It was a brain haemorrhage, mercifully quick. She was 36 years old. Her grave is in the British cemetery at Ooty.

My uncle Peter Bunn, brother of Stanford, was by good luck in India when our little party arrived. He was serving as an officer in the British army and was quick to offer help. Years after the War, he wrote a memoir of his time in India which his daughter, Vanessa Whigham has given to me. It gives a real sense of what it was like being there at that time.

Major Peter N Bunn, Royal Scots and later King's Own Scottish Borderers was the youngest brother of my father Stanford. There were two other brothers, Charles and Henry. The family had lived in South Africa for many years but had close ties with the UK, and several of the children were educated in England.

In the early years of World War II, Peter found himself fighting with his regiment in France, eventually going through the struggles and horrors of the Dunkirk evacuation, which he was lucky to survive. The following year, he was seconded to service in India, which was, as stated above, very fortunate for us.

Ursula with her youngest three children, 1941

He remained in active service after the war, serving in the Far East, and retired in 1952. He married Helen and they settled down in Camberley with their daughter Vanessa and the Burns and the Bunns would meet up from time to time. Vanessa married John Whigham and they now live in London, as do their two adult children, Tristram and Venetia

Stanford changed his name to Burn in 1928, after marrying Ursula in 1929, because he took a dislike to the name Bunn, saying that it might stop him from getting a promotion. He seemed to think the name Burn sounded more distinguished.

Peter Bunn did much to help us at this critical time and deserves our thanks. Elsewhere in his memoir, he describes having had a dream about our journey and our need for his help, long before the actual news reached him. He must have been a very spiritual person. When I last saw him, in about 1985, he was still his charming and very kind self, interested in all our lives since those days in India. A truly fine and loveable man.

He also wrote this simple little tribute to our mother, that I find intensely moving:

A SMALL TRIBUTE TO MY SISTER IN LAW, URSULA

Full marks to Ursula Burn (nee Russell) my eldest brother Stanford's wife, who by her indomitable courage miraculously evacuated with her three children to

India, just before the fall of Hong Kong in 1941.

Carrying Christopher, her small son barely two in her arms and dragging along by their hands her two girls (valiantly assisted by her friend Rachel Harland), Lucinda and Caroline, the two plucky women, severely handicapped as they were, hedge-hopped by plane and sea from Hong Kong to the Tenasserim province of Burma. Tenasserim is that long and narrow strip of Burma in the extreme South East whose strategic importance at the time was owed to the string of airfields constructed there as part of the air reinforcements route between India and Singapore.

Ursula with her small family alternating between walk, road transport and small passenger-carrying planes, struggled bravely up the Tenasserim peninsula to the temporary safety of Moulmein with the advancing Japanese almost at their heels, bombing and strafing the airstrips. My niece Lucinda, her elder girl, remembered these unpleasant incidents which gave her recurrent nightmares for some time. However, Ursula undaunted covering some several thousand miles, landed them safely at Ootacamund, Southern India.

Alas, that horrendous ordeal took its toll and in 1942 she died in Ooty. But may I say that she was a truly brave and courageous woman who by her tremendous determination not only saved the lives of her children but what's more, saved them from the horrors of a Japanese prison camp which that only too recent showing on Television of TENKO, well brought home to the British public for the first time. Jolly well done Ursula. She was only about 36. What rotten luck. Poor girl.

Peter Bunn always said that he had felt guided from some sort of high power to help the children of his sister in law, Ursula. I have always thought that God works through other people. Throughout my life there have been several strong and totally admirable people who have been there to help in times of great need. I was helped by each of them in some way. The power of their example in the way they lived their lives and their moral stance and standards that they set themselves were hugely influential. I learnt from each of them. I sometimes fell short in putting what I learnt into practice. Nevertheless, these people somehow ensured that I always knew the right thing to do in any situation, though regrettably I did not always do it. Peter Bunn was the first of these influencers. From him, I learnt the value of kindness.

Chapter 4

Cometh The Hour - Peter Bunn's Memoir

Thus, did I learn how existence could be cherished,
Strengthened, and fed without the aid of joy (E Brontë)

Extract from a memoir written by Major P N Bunn, younger brother of Stanford Burn, a British Army officer serving in India at the time.

My eldest brother Stanford's wife had died of a cerebral haemorrhage in Ootacamund, Nilgiri Hills, the celebrated blue hills of Southern India.

Henry (another brother), had further advised my going at once to Ooty: to see what could be done to chase up the safe passage home of the three Burn children marooned there, back to England.

We had all so recently been knocked sideways by the horrendous holocaust of the fall of Hong Kong which had claimed so many British lives including her own husband's. Now this. It was simply unbelievable. Again, we were knocked off our pins and rendered speechless and senseless by this double body blow.

I quickly obtained a few days leave from a very sympathetic commandant of the Indian RMA to journey down to Ooty.

Greatly distressed and not feeling in the best of health, I crossed India's sun-scorched baking plains passing through the states of Madras and Mysore. The sun's fierce relentless heat almost boiling me alive, I eventually arrived at the Mattapolyam, foot of the Nilgiri's, my morale in my boots (after changing trains at Coimbatore). I suppose it must have been the end of August beginning of

September 1942.

I stayed the night at the railway terminus at Mattapolyam in a local Dak bungalow surrounded by dense belts of thick almost impenetrable jungle abounding with tiger and other big game such as the Nilgiri Sambhur – a huge antelope (to my regret I shot one of these gorgeous beasts a few years later at Saugor Central Provinces). I well remember the heat was stifling. After a 'gussel' or bath taken in a galvanised tin tub with cans of iced beer to hand, I began to feel a little better.

I was self-contained complete with valise and bedding roll which only had to be spread out over the Indian charpoy bed provided.

I was devastated and shattered thinking of those poor orphaned kids. After supper I crawled into bed under the mosquito net and sank into an exhausted sleep. I emphasise this because It was during this particular night that I had a recurrence of one of my strange mystical dreams.This time I dreamed that I was in a beautiful garden seated at a tea table being given tea by my sister-in-law, Ursula, together with her three children, Lucinda aged about seven, Caroline five and Christopher aged about three. Ursula was bubbling over with high spirits looking happy, strangely young and pretty. She told me not to worry, the kids were perfectly alright. I woke up the following morning feeling strangely refreshed, confident and cheerful.

However, after having breakfasted on Chota Hazri I found myself climbing aboard the first funny little puff puff train with its engine at the back, struggling up the extremely steep and tortuous gradients slowly gramping our way to Ootacamund.

It was an incredible climb of some seven thousand feet or more above the plains. On our arrival I was struck dumb by the sheer beauty of the place. There was an invigorating spicy nip in the air, with a taste of Switzerland. One's spirits were uplifted, and one wanted to dance and sing. The contrast after the hot plains was exhilarating. There was a magnificent panorama of gentian blue-tinted topped hills carpeted in the valleys and up on the slopes by clumps of blue gums and eucalyptus trees giving off intoxicating scents. It strongly reminded me of the rolling Savannah country in South Africa and a bit of the Sussex downs thrown in. The change of light would cast extraordinary, electric blue, purply shadows across the hills. There were delightful English cottages nestling cosily in the folds of the downs each surrounded by their English gardens. It was breath-takingly lovely.

I was met at the station by Rachel Harland, Ursula's great friend. They had evacuated out together before the fall of Hong Kong.

Apparently poor Ursula had had a hair-raising journey through Burma struggling up the Tenasserim and Maymu peninsula with the Japs in hot pursuit. In some instances, according to Rachel they only just managed to escape capture. Poor little Lucinda suffered from recurring nightmares for several years to come.

Ursula had settled down well until death had tragically struck her down. The children were in the care of a Mrs French Rachel had been marvellously kind and had put me up in her bungalow. living close by Rachel. She had obtained a British nanny who attended to their personal needs. That afternoon Rachel had all the kids over to meet their uncle. No sooner after introductions had we sat down to tea when I was overwhelmingly hit by the now familiar intense feeling of deja-vu. I had never seen the children before, until then and they were exactly as pictured in my dream the night before, in features and looks. It was an uncanny coincidence of resemblance, call it what you like. Her spirit had not only welcomed me to Ooty but must have been hovering over her children

Poor Rachel's husband Hector Harland of the Royal Scots, one of Stanford's best friends, had been taken prisoner at the fall of Hong Kong and was in a prison camp at Stanley on the island.

I did everything I could to hasten the departure to the UK of the children to where they were to be cared for and looked after by their grandfather, the Hon B Russell here in Camberley, at Silverwood, Crawley Ridge, who was waiting anxiously for their return.

I worked on Mrs French towards this end. I also had lunch with the Governor of Madras province then luckily in residence at Government House, Ooty, Sir Arthur and Lady Hope, who most kindly offered all the help they could to assist Mrs French, brushing aside much red tape. Everybody had been most kind and helpful, especially poor Rachel who was undergoing fearful agonies herself worrying herself sick over her Hector.

Having tied everything up within my limited scope as best I could in the circumstances, I thanked everyone profusely feeling confident that I had done my best and that the children would be speeded on their way home. Time had run out and I had to make haste in order to return to the RMA and get on with my own life.

In concluding this bittersweet episode in my life there is no doubt that Ursula had died in an earthly paradise or the nearest approach to one representative to a virtual Garden of Eden. A Valhalla. The only other heavenly spot by any comparison that I visited during my brief tour of India was of course Kashmir. The sheer beauty of the place took your breath away. Our oils of Kashmir barely do justice to the almost indescribable loveliness of the country.

Finally, I have construed a little commemorative inscription to Ursula's memory, as enclosed: PNR.

Chapter 5

Under The Luftwaffe - Margie's Childhood

The larks, still bravely singing, fly
Scarce heard amid the guns below (McCrae)

These pages contain a lot about me and not enough about Margie. Sadly, she is at present unable to give her own account of the events of the past eighty years. I have tried to find out as much as possible from other family members and her letters and other writings. I summarise her early life here, as best I can.

When the twins, Margie and Francie were born in Colchester in March 1940, the country was experiencing dire times. The war with Germany was going badly and the whole population must have been feeling stressed and fearful. The following months would see most of the British army return from Dunkirk and the start of the Blitz.

Margie and Francie had two elder sisters – Deirdre (nine years their senior) and Sally (five years their senior). A few years later, their brother David was born.

The twins' first few years were probably therefore spent in an atmosphere with much potential for both sibling rivalry and general insecurity. They seem to have responded by developing considerable inner strength and resilience which was to stand them both in good stead in the future.

Margie and Francie, Crepping, 1945

In the early part of the war, they spent some months in the relative peace and quiet of Galloway in Southern Scotland, staying with Reid relations in Moniaive, which Margie remembers as a nice period in their childhood. Compared to wartime life in Colchester - an army garrison town which is directly under the flight path of any German bombers heading for London, it must have seemed very nice indeed.

The twins were born in a big house in Lexden Road, Colchester but their parents may have wanted to move outside the town to avoid the bombing. However, Ronnie Reid held an important post as surgeon at the hospital throughout the war and needed to be available at short notice. So they stayed. The house at Lexden Road was converted after the war, into a nursing home.

The outbreak of war in September 1939, posed immediate threats to the town and its inhabitants. Colchester was vulnerable to air attack, owing to the vital role of its engineering industries in the war effort and due to its military importance as a garrison town. The town was also on the flight path for enemy bombers on their journeys to and from London and this often led to stray or unused bombs being jettisoned onto the fields surrounding the town.

Being a major army garrison town, there would be up to 40,000 troops stationed there at times. This could bring threats of a different kind:

Christmas Eve 1941: Tonight, took the evening off, although there was much to be done, and went to see a Marx Brothers film at the Playhouse. The streets were packed with howling mobs of soldiers and ATS girls (Auxiliary Territorial Service). Everywhere one saw drunken soldiers sprawling on the pavements, or reeling along, singing. Army lorries were going slowly up the High Street, collecting those men who were quite incapable. The inert bodies were being heaved over tail boards, respirators and tin-helmets following with a metallic crash. I noticed the civil police kept well in the background. (From the wartime diary of E J Rudsdale, Curator, Colchester Museum).

But apart from this, Colchester's geographic position as first defence against air, sea or land attack by Germany, meant it was in an almost constant state of alert during the war.

Colchester Blitz: Air raid sirens sounded over 1000 times in Colchester during the course of the war. Colchester was attacked by the Luftwaffe on several occasions, including: Severalls Raid – On 11 August 1942 38 citizens were killed when a German plane dropped a stick of bombs on Severalls Hospital. Chapel Street Raid – 8 citizens were killed when a Dornier 217 dropped four bombs on South Street and Essex Street on 28 September 1942. The air raid siren, in this case, only sounded after the bombs had already dropped, causing outcry in the town. St Botolphs Raid – In February 1944 a large Luftwaffe firebombing raid dropped a stream of 1,400 incendiary bombs on the St Botolphs area of the town, destroying 14 buildings and seriously damaging 99 others. Two-thirds of the Paxman Britannia Works was destroyed during the raid. (Wikipedia).

After the war ended, the Reid children lived at Crepping Hall, a lovely old manor house going back to the Domesday Book of 1068, and reputedly haunted. In fact, Margie remembers her mother complaining a lot about the ghosts and what a nuisance they were, and citing them as a reason for going to live somewhere else. This the family eventually did, after about eight years in residence.

Margie and Francie knew the house backwards and would sometimes hide in the bedrooms and later come out with stories of what they observed. Margie wrote about all this years later, on a website that featured the history of Crepping Hall:

My parents moved to Crepping in 1946, from Colchester, it was an utterly wonderful new life for me and my twin, we were 6 years old, and had been townies in Colchester! The farmer was so kind, he allowed us to feed his pigs, and taste the pig food, and, when we were a bit older, to ride on the backs of his Suffolk Punch horses, All around were lovely woods for us to run in with our dogs. So many trees and haystacks to climb too, it was perfect! No wonder there are so many children who remember what a wonderful place it was.
One of the best times, as 'wild childs' at Crepping, was when there was a usual houseful of guests at week-ends. We, the twins, left them all, to climb in the haystacks in a barn: Whilst we were there, two of the guests came in, and the man went down on one knee and proposed to my mother's cousin, in the traditional manner, as we watched, silently, from above! We then rushed home, and reenacted the scene to the rest of the house party! Little beasts as we must have been, it ended well. They married and lived happily ever after.
Margaret Burn (Nèe Reid) November 2013.

Perhaps unsurprisingly, the twins were sent off to boarding school at an early age. Margie loved her time at New Hall, then a relatively small girls-only, convent school near Chelmsford, where she and Francie went as boarders in 1954. Perhaps because their parents were to go through a divorce in 1959, they found the boarding school with its devoted community of nuns, a place of calm and safety where they could express themselves and develop. Today, New Hall is a much larger place, for boys and girls. The nuns have ceased to be involved and indeed the convent community has removed itself to a house in Colchester.

It is a sign of the fondness that Margie and Francie had for the place, that Francie now lies buried in the nuns' burial ground at New Hall, following her untimely death in 1978.

As they reached their teens, the twins were sent to France in the holidays to stay with (separate) French families to learn the language and generally extend their education. They seem to have had a generally good time and made some nice friends while also fending off the lustful advances of the rather forward young French boys. A bit later, they would both find themselves working in Paris.

Chapter 6

Convoy To Camberley – By Sea To England

Run up the sail, my heartsick comrades;
Let each horizon tilt and lurch (MacNeice)

The fairly good ship Franconia was to carry my sisters and I the fifteen thousand miles from Bombay to London, via Cape Town, South Africa. A cruise liner converted into a troopship at the start of World War II, her best days were well behind her by the time we went aboard, yet she proved equal to the task. At 22,155 tons she was roughly half the size of the Titanic but happily, a lot more seaworthy.

SS Franconia, 1942

To convert a cruise ship into a troopship, you make all the little cabins into several very big cabins and fill them with as many bunk beds as possible. You also make the posh dining room into a canteen and take away the tablecloths. At least that was how it seemed to me when I thought about it later.

For this voyage, there were both troops on board and civilians, including quite a lot of children. We shared a big cabin with some other families, about twenty people together.

Our own little travel group of Lucinda, Caroline and myself were put in charge of a sort of nanny known (by us at any rate) as 'Bangie', perhaps because she was very strict and quite noisy. I don't know her real name. The sea trip from Bombay to England was to take about six weeks and we were pretty fed up with Bangie by the end of it but, in retrospect she must have been a good and responsible person. How all this was arranged, I have no idea.

It may seem a jump in this narrative to go from arrival in India almost directly to departure for Europe, but the truth is that I have no recall whatsoever of the few months that my sisters and I spent at Ooty after our mother died, before embarking on the Franconia. I assume this to mean that the days passed in relative calm and that nothing traumatic or otherwise memorable happened. India is a fascinating place and I certainly wish that I had memories of what it was like, at this very important time in its history and ours.

Anyway, however it came about, we found ourselves one day aboard SS Franconia, sailing out of Bombay harbour, bound for the UK. Our trip would take us across the Indian Ocean and round the Cape of Good Hope (South Africa) and then up into the North Atlantic to home waters and the English Channel. This longer route was used in wartime rather than the shorter one, through the Suez Canal and the Mediterranean, because it was considered less dangerous.

Nevertheless, there were perils everywhere in the form of enemy submarines (U Boats) and later, aircraft and surface ships. Sea travel during the war was almost always done in convoys – only the very fast ships such as the Queen Mary, were able to travel alone because they could outrun almost all the enemy ships. A typical convoy would be a group of merchant and passenger ships sailing in formation, protected by Royal Navy ships, mainly destroyers. There were a lot of casualties in spite of the best efforts of the Navy, largely because the convoy could only travel at the speed of the slowest ship, which rendered them easy targets.

I do have a few memories of this time, but the overriding impression was one of boredom. Here's a typical day on board, as described to me by one of my sisters:

Child: "I want to go outside"
Grown- up: "You can't, it's too rough, you'll get blown away"
Child: "I'm going to be sick:"
Grown-up "You've just been sick. Drink some water"
Child: "I'm going to be sick"
Grown-up: "Here's a bucket."

But the boredom changed to moments of sheer terror when our convoy came under attack. When the siren went on the ship, we would all huddle together on the bunk beds in our big cabin and listen to the guns banging and thumping outside and the planes screeching overhead and men running noisily up and down the steel decks overhead. This happened several times on the voyage and they are the bits I really remember. We would all be wearing life jackets and people would tell us about lifeboat drill and what to do if the ship started to sink. I found it all quite frightening but there were some grown-ups who sat around singing songs and smoking and didn't seem to mind at all. Probably they were just trying to keep everyone's spirits up.

Leaving Bombay in the late summer of 1942 to travel by sea to England was the closing of one chapter in my life. I was leaving behind a world that I would never experience again - Colonial India.

This, (and Hong Kong too for that matter), was a place of huge class difference between the privileged few (mainly the British) and the extreme poor. A place where the master – servant relationship was strictly maintained, and you were 'letting the side down' if you did not comply. I was not of course aware of any of this at the time, being just two years old, but I could later recognise the attitude in the old colonial types that still existed back in the UK in the 1940's and 1950's. The far east was and still is, mostly a far more vibrant, noisy and colourful place than many Western European countries. Certainly, England in 1942 seemed a very dreary place indeed in comparison.

Eventually, our long sea voyage ended, and we reached England – a place I had never seen before. It had not been an enjoyable trip but we had made it home – we had been lucky, because there were many ships that ended up on the bottom of the sea. I have never wanted to go on a cruise or a long sea journey again, and I never have.

Chapter 7

The Master And Chatelaine - Col. Russell And May

As long as I stay in your service, pray,
Don't ever be downhearted (Wilcox)

Colonel Russell was my grandfather – the father of Ursula (my mother), Prudence (my guardian and de facto mother, after the death of Ursula), Joan and Clodagh. He was also the father of Michael by his second marriage. A truly remarkable character and role model. He was a man of very high principles and a disciplinarian. Whenever we met (which would be several times each year) I would shake him by the hand and call him 'Sir'. Failure to do so was unthinkable. He was the youngest son of Sir Charles Russell, Baron Russell of Killowen and Lord Chief Justice of England, who died in 1900.

Bertie as he was known, was in the British Army and served in the South African Boer War in 1900 and in World War II, fighting in France in 1915, where he was wounded and received the DSO. In World War II he apparently tried to join the Home Guard (in his sixties) but was refused on account of an unsuitable attitude (insubordination and his quirky sense of humour).

Bertrand was a keen racegoer and an owner too. I have a photo of him and my mother at Royal Ascot races in 1923.

Bertrand Russell and Ursula, Royal Ascot 1923

After retirement, his great passion as mentioned earlier, was breeding pedigree Shetland Sheepdogs (Shelties) which had the run of his large house and gardens. A least a dozen dogs would be in the house whenever we visited and each of his many grandchildren would have their own particular favourite – mine was a lovely black and white creature called Victor. Grandpa would drive to all the major dog shows in his big American car (a Lincoln Zephyr) with May and the dogs in the back and was a leading breeder and prizewinner.

To say that dogs were more important than children at Silverwood might be an exaggeration, but dogs and children combined, made up a perfect squad to be paraded, disciplined and marched around Camberley common every morning for a couple of hours exercise. During the walk we (dogs included) would be given tasks, intelligence tests and questions on map reading, geography and the like. All quite demanding but hugely beneficial and, dare I say it, enjoyable.

A competitive and critical man, but always in a constructive manner, he would reward you with praise and sometimes even a ten-shilling note, if you gave the right answer. And if you could solve one of the clues in the Times crossword puzzle that he liked to complete every day, then you were made to feel very special indeed.

As I grew older, I began to appreciate this man's wit and wisdom more and more. He died when I was twenty years old and I realised only later, how much I had learnt from him. He was unquestionably the most influential person of my childhood.

From him I learnt the importance of cultivating the mind and body, 'mens sana in corpore sano', and the need to have the right standards to live by. He did not suffer fools gladly, but he would do all he could, to stop you from being a fool.

Grandpa's constant help and companion for at least the last thirty years of his life was his housekeeper, May. She looked after his every personal need and the dogs as well. She was his Nellie Dean and his Sancho Panza combined. She brought common sense and practical results to his plans and she would support him through thick and thin. When Bertie was at home suffering greatly from the cancer that was to kill him, she was at his side through it all. It was an impressive and unforgettable display, and the family did not forget.

May Scott and Alexander, 1968

An outwardly fearsome lady, her heart was pure gold. Her bark was worse than her bite (the doggy reference is appropriate because one of her roles was as chief groomer, trainer, feeder and waterer to the pack of Shelties that were such a feature of life at Silverwood). When these canine tasks were completed, she would switch effortlessly to providing the same services to Colonel Russell and his guests. The kitchen was her absolute fiefdom and all in the house, especially visiting children and their nannies, had better be aware.

She also liked a joke, though her sense of humour took a bit of getting used to. My cousin Andrew Brand tells this story:

"my other memories include swimming at the Blue Pool in Camberley and going to a swimming gala demonstration there. May had told us she would be diving off the highest board and we should look out for her. Of course we did not see her doing that, but when we got back to the house she had a wet swimming costume hanging on the line which she said was evidence that she had taken part, but we had not noticed."

She would loudly berate us all, the Colonel included, for transgressions such as entering the house with dirty shoes but would brook no criticism of us from any outsiders. In defence of the Russell family she was fierce, and her loyalty extended to us all. She really didn't seem to have any family of her own and she continued as the Colonel's housekeeper way beyond retirement age, though in great pain from rheumatism.

Following the Colonel's death, the family bought her a little house in Camberley where she lived very happily for many years. She always enjoyed being visited and getting news of our adventures. A fine example of unconditional love in action. May died in 1980.

Chapter 8

Silverwood – A House Remembered

Footfalls echo in the memory
Down the passage which we did not take (Eliot)

The big house had a huge rhododendron-filled garden, a tennis court and garages (behind which I smoked my first fag and was horribly sick). It had a tiny pond where Caroline fell in on a winter's day, and a grassy bit in the trees where I flattened a neighbour, young Tim Orr, with my first ever golf swing (entirely by mistake, but it caused quite a fuss). The images are much more real than of any house I have lived in since.

Silverwood does not exist anymore. After my grandfather died in 1960, it was sold to a developer who pulled down the big house and built several smaller houses in the grounds. But in my memory, I can still go into every room and see the furniture, the paintings on the walls and the china ornaments (Meissen, Dresden, Sevres), the carpets and chintz curtains, with perfect clarity. I don't know why this is so – perhaps because it was the first English house that I ever saw. And certainly, between the ages of two and nineteen, I spent a considerable amount of time there.

When I first met Grandpa, he was already sixty-three and very set in his ways. He had lived there a long time and since his second wife was sadly put in a secure nursing home many years beforehand, he and his redoubtable housekeeper, May had established a routine that seldom varied. Meals were always on time and announced by a brass gong in the hall. The day followed a strict timetable of dog walking, Times crossword, Camberley Bridge Club, and perhaps further card games after dinner.

Burn children, Siverwood, 1943

It has long been a joke in my family that very wealthy people, when they invite you to their houses, like to keep you waiting in some elegant downstairs room in order to give you the opportunity to admire their many possessions. At Silverwood, this was impossible because as soon as the front door opened, the visitor would be overwhelmed by a mass of dogs closely followed by my grandfather, cursing them fluently.

We children had the run of the place as long as we didn't upset the grown-ups.

There were often cousins to play with as well – grandfather's other two daughters had families who would visit regularly: Auntie Joan, wife of Charles Brand who had three children – Andrew, Duncan and Felicity and often visited from London, and Auntie Clo (Clodagh), wife of Colonel (later Brigadier) Tommy Haddon, a serving officer who had a very active war, experiencing Dunkirk, the invasion of Sicily and Arnhem where he was taken prisoner by the Germans. Clo's three boys were Paul, Martin and John.

All these cousins were roughly the same age as us and we all got on pretty well (we all still do, I am glad to say, although Paul and Duncan are very sadly, no longer with us).

This is the house too where I had my first alcohol – Green Chartreuse in a tiny thimble of a glass aged about twelve, I think. How delicious it tasted.

And this is the house where I experienced the war again, sitting wrapped in blankets in May's kitchen at night, as the Luftwaffe dropped thumping great bombs on nearby Aldershot barracks and the whole building shook and the lights flickered.

The children were all scared of May and so were some of the grown-ups. Luckily, she always had a soft spot for me so I would be sent by the others to ask her for biscuits or soap powder (in short supply in wartime) by Auntie Prue. It generally worked – an early exercise in the power of manipulation.

Dogs were everywhere. Shelties are lovely intelligent animals, but they do make a lot of noise and bark at anything and everything, including children. Dogs would lie around on the floor and on some of the furniture too and not everyone was a fan of this, my aunt Joan in particular, was not a dog lover at all. It was grandpa's habit sometimes to throw a tennis ball for the dogs to chase – a game best played outside you might agree. He played it in the drawing room, after dinner, much to the dismay of his many guests. Precious objects were regularly smashed and every valuable piece of porcelain on display bore the scars of this game. Family relationships were also pretty chipped and cracked at times.

The last time I visited Silverwood was in 1960. My grandfather had died a month earlier and the house was almost empty and up for sale. May was moving out to a small house in Camberley and I had come to help her. There was no furniture, no dogs, no voices. In a corner of the empty drawing room I found a broken piece of a china plate, beautifully decorated but damaged beyond repair. I put it in my pocket and still have it today.

Chapter 9

A New Life – Yorkshire And Auntie Prue

To lose and start again at your beginnings
And never breathe a word about your loss (Kipling)

I can't recall exactly when it sunk in that I (with my sisters) was an orphan, but when the realisation hit me, it hurt. Being chased round the Far East by the Japs may have been unpleasant but it seemed somehow manageable and didn't last that long. Being orphaned on the other hand, seemed a disastrous life sentence and very, very personal. Far too personal to talk about with anyone, my sisters included. So, I never did. At least not until I had therapy at the age of forty-six.

It wasn't all bad. Our father may have died, and our mother too, but we got the next best thing, in the form of our mother's sister, Prudence. The eldest of Colonel Russell's four daughters, Prudence was the most unconventional. A trained actress, she had been married and divorced before she took us on, and she had no children of her own. When I think of her now, I feel nothing but very deep affection. But in 1942, I and my sisters were a lot more ambivalent.

During the years that were to come, this high principled and wholly admirable lady made us her priority, sacrificing a great deal along the way including a promising stage career. I have absolutely no doubt that she did her absolute best to live up to the promise given to her beloved sister Ursula before she departed to Hong Kong – that she would look after the children if anything bad happened. She did indeed do her best, yet for all her efforts, it still didn't feel quite the same.

Prue, Gordon and the Burns, 1953

At first, I think we were all quite suspicious and our emotions were not in a good state anyway, so it's not surprising that I remember our early times in Yorkshire as difficult and rather drab. Yet this was where Auntie Prue, as we were to call her, had been living and where we were to start our new life.

Everything suddenly seemed to slow down when we got to her little cottage in Hampsthwaite, near Harrogate in the Yorkshire dales. Even saying the word 'Hampsthwaite' with its six juxtaposed consonants, seems to slow you down. Auntie Prue would drive us to and from our primary schools in her tiny Austin Seven car, nicknamed 'Greenie' (guess its colour) and we would go for little walks afterwards, or play in the garden or visit other families nearby for tea and jam and margarine sandwiches while World War II rumbled inexorably on in the far distance, almost unnoticed.

In the school holidays we would all cram into Greenie and meander uncomfortably down the A1 to Camberley where Grandpa, May and the dogs would welcome us to a rather more challenging but hugely enjoyable, experience.

To my shame, I don't think that I ever gave any thought to the effect that events must have had on Auntie Prue, who had lost a cherished sister and taken on a life-changing new role with constant cheerfulness and not a single word of complaint. She probably missed her life as an actress.

I have inserted below an extract from the London Stage, a publication that lists all London theatre productions. This extract from 1924 shows Prudence Russell appearing at Her Majesty's Theatre in a play by George Grossmith (creator of Mr Pooter) alongside the great Yvonne Arnaud, among others. It must have been a proud moment although there appear to have been only nine performances.

The London Stage

34.329 The Royal Visitor (George Grossmith and J. Solano) adpt. Of Robert de Flers and Gaston-Arman de Caillavet Le Roi 1908. HIS MAJESTY'S 27/9/24-4/10/24. 9 perf. Boudier - Oscar Asche, Rivelot - Anew McMaster, Sernin de Chamarande - Denys Blakelock, Cruchet - Leonard Calvert, Blond - George Grossmith, Suzette - Zoe Palmer, Marthe - Yvonne Arnaud, Georgette - Prudence Russell, Francine - Dorothy Field....

Prudence trained at RADA. Appearing on the London stage then, as now, was a huge achievement. She appeared in several London productions before going to Harrogate, Yorkshire to join the White Rose Players.

At the start of the War, in 1939, Prue had left the stage and volunteered for war work as a VAD (Voluntary Aid Detachment). This was a unit of civilians providing auxiliary nursing care, mostly in hospitals. Many people from an arts background did this sort of wartime work, including Hattie Jacques and Agatha Christie. Perhaps they enjoyed dressing up in Nurses uniforms which were very different in those days to what nurses wear now. The VADs were nicknamed 'The Starched Brigade'. But it was hard and often harrowing work and Prue used to tell us stories of long hours with wounded soldiers at local hospitals.

In September 1948, seven years old, I started my first term as a boarder at preparatory school, and a lot of changes followed from this. In 1951 Prue married again, to Gordon Findlay, an interior decorator with an upmarket clientele, who no doubt brought her a lot of happiness, though his appearance brought conflict for us children. Prue was often torn between meeting his needs and ours.

Chapter 10

The Lion Of Whitby – Miss Longhorn

I came home and found a lion in my living room –
rushed out on the fire escape screaming Lion! Lion! (Ginsberg)

Ada Longhorn, or Nanny Longhorn as we called her, came into our lives in about 1948 and stayed until she died about 35 years later. Outwardly quiet and mousy, strangers sometimes thought her un-assertive. But they were quite wrong. Outwardly, butter (actually, margarine in the 1940's) wouldn't melt in her mouth. So much so, that my sister Jancis ironically christened her, "the Lion of Whitby", but this was not meant unkindly. Everyone knew that you didn't mess with Nanny Longhorn, if there was an important principle at stake. You might think on first acquaintance, that she was a bit quiet, at worst a bit of a doormat, but this was not so. She was always highly determined in doing whatever she felt was right.

She came from Whitby, the lovely little fishing town near Scarborough on the East Yorkshire coast. It had once been a place of importance with a famous abbey. Miss Longhorn, as a young girl, had worked for the nuns at Whitby abbey, whom she said were very demanding employers. Yet sometimes she would go back to Whitby for a short holiday and she would stay with the nuns at the abbey.

Her father had been a sea captain and her sister Mary still lived in the charmingly-named Ugglebarnby, a tiny village outside Whitby – married to a local farmer called Norman, a through and through Yorkshireman and a kind man. As small children, we would have holidays on the farm and helped feed the animals and sit on the great shire horses that were still doing the ploughing work in the fields there. Mary and Norman would go to a lot of trouble to give us a nice time and we all enjoyed these outings.

With Norman, Ugglebarnby, 1947

Nanny was a very meek and kindly person. I can't remember seeing her angry or raising her voice. She was not physically very strong, but she tried to do everything and was unfailingly devoted to helping our little family through thick and thin. She also set great store by education, perhaps because her own had been fairly basic, and she encouraged us to work and led the way herself. She liked to read books of history and self-improvement and passed on this to us all.

She and I once composed a song (or rather put new words to an old song we used to sing at bedtime, the one that goes:

Now the day is over,
Night is drawing nigh;
Shadows of the evening
Steal across the sky.
Jesus, give the weary
Calm and sweet repose;
With Thy tend'rest blessing
May mine eyelids close. Etc...

Which we turned into:

Now the bath is over,
Supper's drawing nigh.
Milk and bread and butter
Down the stairs I spy.
Lucinda and Caroline
Always get there first.
I am in the bathroom
Putting on my shirt....

She was another of those people who came into my life without my being aware quite how, but who was an absolute power for good. Nanny was a regular churchgoer and I doubt that she ever had a bad thought in her life. I cannot imagine her telling a lie either.

When we were children, Nanny Longhorn would come with us on our trips to stay with grandfather at Silverwood. Here the routine, even in the 1950's was so attuned to the pre-war era, that nannies were automatically relegated to the servants' quarters. Thus, Nanny Longhorn would spend her time, when not with us, hobnobbing with May the housekeeper and any other nannies that other visitors had brought with them. This must have presented her with special challenges because there were a whole lot of protocols here that she would have had to learn, and May was not an easy person to get along with. Still, she never complained and indeed kept her end up in asserting her position in the housekeeping hierarchy.

After we all grew up, Nanny Longhorn lived in a little cottage in Spofforth, Yorkshire, near to Prue and Gordon. She was very fond of Margie and the children and would come to visit us wherever we were living. She came out to Malta and with her family's seafaring background, she loved going round the Grand Harbour looking at all the ships and the Naval depots. When we lived in London she would come, and we would take her on boat trips down the river to Greenwich – still a remarkable experience for anyone

She loved going to church and singing hymns – her favourite was John Bunyan's 'To Be a Pilgrim' – a great choice.

Who would true valour see, Let him come hither;
One here will constant be, Come wind, come weather.
There's no discouragement Shall make him once relent

His first avowed intent, To be a pilgrim.....

The last time I saw the Lion of Whitby, she was most unwell and in hospital. Though she recognised me, she was thoroughly confused as to where she was and what was happening. Yet she was laughing about it all and seemed to have accepted that the end was coming.

She had a simple funeral at Spofforth, and she is buried close to Prue and Gordon with whom most of her adult life had been linked. [illegible] and Mary came to the funeral and we had a nice chat about days long gone by, at the farm in Ugglebarnby.

I think she saw her whole life as a form of pilgrimage, a road to be travelled, where one met other pilgrims whom one would try to help, to the best of one's ability.

What a great pilgrim she herself turned out to be. And what a lion.

Chapter 11

The Power Of Example - The Brands And The Haddons

Oh, what a lantern, what a lamp of light
Is thy pure word to me
To clear my paths and guide my goings right! (Herbert)

It says a lot for the bond that existed between the four Russell girls, that when Ursula tragically died, the remaining three immediately rallied round – Prue taking the role of guardian and her sisters Joan Brand and Clodagh Haddon taking a keen interest and doing all they could to help.

Having strong role models when you are young is very important. I have been lucky. My mother's side of the family (the Russell side) played a huge part in my upbringing (my father's side – the Bunns, were mostly in South Africa and thus far less involved).

As children, we saw a lot of our cousins. Joan was married to Charles Brand, head of a large Civil Engineering company. They and their three children Andrew, Duncan and Felicity lived in London, and also had a cottage at Hillhead, on the coast between Portsmouth and Southampton.

The Brands loved small boats and we had many active and exciting holidays with them sailing and sometimes racing in their little sailing dinghies on the Solent. This was one of Britain's busiest sea areas at the time because Southampton was the main port for transatlantic travel and we would have the almost daily sight of the great liners – Queen Elizabeth, Queen Mary, United States and lots of others arriving and departing along Southampton water. Opposite too was

Cowes on the Isle of Wight where large yachts would gather in the summer. It was the ideal kind of holiday for us and Uncle Charles, Joan's husband was a kind and energetic man who always had something planned for us. One night there was a summer storm and he insisted we all had a midnight swim, to have something to remember - and we did. Though, I think Auntie Joan stayed in bed.

The Russell girls, 1914

At other times, we would go to stay with the Haddons, who lived near Haslemere. Uncle Tommy was a much-decorated army officer who was very efficient and also very kind. We did a lot of camping, sometimes in their large garden. I remember one night when we decided to sleep indoors for a change, my tent was left in the garden and got stolen during the night. I was quite upset because I really liked camping (still do). But Uncle Tommy went off quietly to London and bought me another one the next day. He was that sort of man.

Tommy was a professional soldier who had an amazingly tough but by no means untypical, experience of World War ll. Here is a description by my cousin, Andrew Brand:

"Tommy was a regular officer in the Border Regiment, and he and Clodagh were married in Camberley very soon after war was declared. He had then gone to France at the outbreak of war with the First Battalion of his regiment which formed part of the British Expeditionary Force, only to return via Dunkirk in May – June 1940 after Germany had invaded France via Belgium, in the

Blitzkrieg.

After some further time with the Battalion re-forming in the UK Tommy went to the Staff College at Camberley for a three months course (during which he and Clodagh lodged at Silverwood), and was then given a job at the War Office in London as a Secretary to the Joint Intelligence Committee. He happened to be the Duty Officer at the Cabinet offices the night in December 1941 when the Japanese attacked Pearl Harbour, so bringing the USA into the war, and had to pass on the news to No. 10. During this time Tommy and Clodagh (and Paul, born about November 1940) lived in a flat in Paultons Square, just off the King's Road in Chelsea.

In about February 1943 Tommy returned to regimental soldiering as second in command of 1 Border and in April 1943 the Battalion, now part of a newly formed Air Landing Brigade (i.e. the men were to arrive on their objective by Glider, not Parachute) was moved to North Africa with a view to the start of the Italian campaign. This began in July with the invasion of Sicily. The airborne element of this was marred by missed targets and about 60% of the gliders, including Tommy's, landed in the sea and he had to swim four miles to get ashore. His battalion was withdrawn to North Africa to recover and re-equip but then went back to Taranto when the mainland of Italy was invaded in September. Tommy was now C O in the rank of Lieutenant Colonel. The battalion continued to fight up the East coast of Italy but were withdrawn to North Africa and home to UK in December 1943 to prepare for invasion of Europe.

Although for the Normandy invasion on D Day in June 1944 gliders were used for the capture of Pegasus Bridge, the Air Landing Brigade of which Tommy and 1 Border formed part was held in reserve and did not go into action until they went to Arnhem in September in Operation Market Garden. As you will know this was a disaster and although he was lucky enough to survive, Tommy was taken prisoner and remained in German hands until the end of the war."

Charles Brand had also joined the army at the start of the war but was soon dispatched to take over running the family Civil engineering company that was a vital part of the war effort. That did not put him out of danger however as he continued to live in London, performing night-time fire watching duties. He had some narrow escapes:

Charles meanwhile remained in London. From the time of his release from the Army his war work had been Fire Watching as a volunteer in the evenings and overnight. He came down to Silverwood at weekends and other occasions when he could get away. One night, after an evening spent at his Club, he was walking home when knocked flat by a bomb blast, but fortunately was not seriously hurt. It turned out that a Doodle Bug has come down at our end of the Fulham Road and the blast had blown out the front door and all the windows at 12 Pelham Place. It was fortunate that the house was empty because the beds in our so-called air raid shelter were full of the glass blown out from the windows!

During the war, and for the first few years after it, Charles kept chickens in the back garden of 12 Pelham Place. At first six in one shed built by CB&S plant yard staff, but a second shed was added later, and the numbers doubled. They were fed on a brew made in the kitchen of domestic scraps to which special stuff was added to make the shells of their eggs hard. They provided eggs which supplemented the ration and when their laying days were over their necks were wrung and they were cooked and eaten. Friends and family contributed scraps and received eggs in return. Charles cleaned out the sheds every morning before going to the office and buried the muck in the flower beds.

After the War, in August 1952, I went with the Haddons – Clodagh and Tommy and their three boys Paul, Martin and John, on a camping trip to a farm in Devon, at Lynmouth. The weather was appalling, and it rained night and day, though Uncle Tommy's military skills meant that we kept safe and dry. But the next morning we heard that the little town, only a short distance away, had been badly flooded and cars and whole houses had been swept away. 34 people died that night.

These wonderful aunts, uncles and cousins brought a whole new dimension into our young lives and we learnt an awful lot from them, that we might not have learnt from Auntie Prue. Sailing, camping and golfing are some of the things they introduced me to. And I had people to play cricket with as well.

The Brands and the Haddons continued to be a big influence for many years. Though Joan and Charles and Clodagh and Tommy have departed this life, and Duncan Brand and Paul Haddon are sadly gone too, I think of them all with great affection and gratitude. And it is still an absolute pleasure to see my cousins Andrew and Felicity (though Felicity lives in America) and Martin and John and their respective families.

A colleague at work happened to say to me the other day: "the only thing that really matters in life are your relationships to other people". I agree completely.

Chapter 12

The Shock Of School – Gilling Castle And Ampleforth College

There we met with famous men, sat in office o'er us
And they beat on us with rods (Kipling)

Harry Potter has done a lot for the image of boarding schools and for all I know, every boarding child today does have a lovely exciting time, getting up to all sorts of pranks while socking it to the school bully. But it wasn't quite like that in my day.

In post-war-austerity Britain, where just about everything was rationed except Snoek (revolting tinned fish sent to Britain by the South Africans, presumably because they hated the sight of it), boarding school was not much fun. From the very first day it seemed an alien experience and it stayed like that for most of the next ten years. But that didn't stop me engaging in the process. I became head boy and won a scholarship.

There were seventy-odd boys aged from seven to twelve at Gilling Castle, the preparatory school for Ampleforth College. I doubt that even half of them enjoyed the boarding school experience. A cold and draughty seven hundred-year-old castle (with some later additions) may be a thing of historical interest to some people, but it does not lend itself well to meeting the needs of a large group of very young and often emotionally fragile children. Added to which, the various Benedictine monks and lay staff seemed singularly unsuited, with very few exceptions, to either managing or teaching. Small children deserve better than to be minded by men dressed in long black robes, such as worn by the angel of death.

Nevertheless, I did have some good times there. Children are very resilient. I enjoyed the sports, the outings to the lakes and even some of the lessons. I won a prize for Latin and another prize for History. I made a speech to the school. I learnt to swim, play rugby and cricket. Mr Lorrigan, the wacky Irishman who taught games and music (an unusual combination), said I could "run like a deer".

The time came to move on. Across the valley in clear sight were the imposing buildings of Ampleforth College, the big school. I was now twelve years old.

I can't remember saying goodbye and thank you to Gilling but I suppose I did – they were pretty expert at beating good manners into their charges.

If Gilling Castle had been shocking and sometimes brutal, Ampleforth the 'big school', provided a more varied experience. There were indeed many moments of exquisite elegance and intellectual excellence at this school that I have seldom known the like of, since leaving. At such times I felt stimulated and I felt special. A school that allows a chosen few, of which I was one, to sit comfortably around an oaken table in an elegantly panelled study, quoting and composing Greek poetry on a regular basis, does that for you.

Our Classics Master, Philip Smiley was a legend. He would treat us in a very grown-up way, as if we were already at university, and expect us to work on our own, produce essays and then read them out to him in tutorials. It didn't always work well, but we liked his approach. I was sometimes quite short of time to do homework because of my commitment to the school Rugby team, especially when there were away matches which really cut the amount of time available for study. When it came to tutorial time, I was often unprepared and hit on the wheeze of making up my essays on the spot – spouting them off the top of my head rather than reading out a previously-written piece. Needless to say, this didn't work, and Philip Smiley always knew. But he never imposed any kind of punishment. It all felt very mature and sophisticated but actually, what I really needed was to learn some proper discipline.

In the sixth form I was a 'Monitor', an official with special powers and privileges which allowed us to organise the younger boys and occasionally, to chastise them. We had our own common room where we could make tea and toast and sit around a large table discussing the behaviour of various troublemakers in a supposedly civilised manner. It was hoped that this sort of routine would equip us to become leaders of men in later life and give us a sense of responsibility.

But when you are later sitting round that table watching one of your peers, usually the head boy, bending a smaller boy over the back of a chair and beating him mercilessly with a cane, these pious intentions, in my case at any rate, become very questionable. Luckily, in my time at Ampleforth, I never had to beat any boy, though I was myself beaten several times. It was not an experience easily forgotten

When I first arrived in the big school, I was low down in the pecking order. At that time, it had over five hundred boys grouped into eight different houses; all of which had different characteristics: St Cuthbert's for example, was run by Fr Walter Maxwell Stuart, scion of an ancient Scottish family. The boys here tended to be the sons of the landed gentry who were encouraged to try field sports (Ampleforth had its own pack of beagles at that time). St Dunstan's, where I was placed, seemed to be a mixture of boys from all backgrounds – no bad thing.

Fr Oswald and St Dunstan's monitors, 1959

Fr. Oswald Vanheems, the housemaster of St Dunstan's House, was not a very outgoing or particularly loveable person. He did not speak a lot, quite a welcome attribute in one whose body language oozed disapproval. He was known as a strict disciplinarian. He was however a basically good and devout man with high standards and high principles, and he prioritised the welfare of the boys in his charge. Difficult to deal with on a personal level, his heart was in the right place as they say, and I gradually came to like him, over the four years that I was there.

Poor Fr Oswald, he was very set in his ways. His study was next to the House common room, a place where we could play 'nice' records on the gramophone. Perhaps even Ella Fitzgerald or Frank Sinatra. But in 1956, Rock Around The Clock hit the UK, followed by Elvis, and all hell broke loose very quickly indeed. There were riots in the cinemas and young people suddenly were in the news. I was sixteen and very much aware of it all. But nobody had told Fr Oswald. I suppose Benedictine monasteries weren't quick in getting that sort of news. Anyway, I came back to school after the holidays with a trunkful of rock and roll records, as did lots of other people and one day we put one on the record player in Fr Oswald's room. I think it was Elvis doing Hound Dog. He hit the roof and for me it was another black mark.

Chapter 13

Letters Of Credit - Margie's Teenage Missives

Life is full of froth and bubble - two things stand alone.
Kindness in another's trouble, courage in your own (Anon)

Margie used to have the above little ditty on the wall beside her bed - and she has most certainly followed its message throughout her life.

Reids and Luggs, Scotland, 1949

While I was adjusting to life's challenges in Camberley, Yorkshire and then boarding school, Margie was going through a similar process in Essex where her home life probably became increasingly difficult, culminating in her parents' divorce in 1959. She and Francie spent several years at New Hall School, near Chelmsford. Later they stayed with families in France to improve their French and after school days, they were both in shared flats in London.

The twins were great letter writers and Margie's father Ronnie seems to have thought so too because he kept a lot of them, which were later returned to her when Ronnie died.

Here are a few extracts which illustrate Margie's life at the time, better than I could describe. They do her great credit.

New Hall, Chelmsford
17th March 1955

Darling Daddy,
I hope you are fine. I have just risen from my bed of sickness where I lay with a slight temp and a loud rattle in my chest for four days. I am better, but at times, I still sound like Grandpa mounting the stairs. Dr Stone, who came and listened, sends you his regards.

Sam S has also sent you them. He has been staying here. Ever so jolly. I think the proverb "empty vessels...." suits him admirably at times. Poor Christa has had an ugly break, she has trotted off to hospital to have her elbow sliced. She was very nervous before she went, poor thing.

We won a match yesterday 22 - nil! The other side must have been rotten! The swimming pool was opened today - the priest blessed it and then Reverend Mother tipped in a bottle of Champagne and about ten of us leapt in. I did a really first-class bellyflop, the water parted like the Red Sea for the Israelites and my stomach was red and sore. Everyone stood enviously on the brink....
The French Oral is on 10th April, and I am busy parleying Francais.
Well very much love to you and everyone. Could we have some stamps - this is our last!
Margie

Then a bit later, she writes a very sweet letter when her father is obviously struggling with the breakup of his marriage and feeling guilty about its affect on the family;

"...Please Daddy don't be sad about not giving your children a happy home. You've given us so much, firstly more luck in food and clothing and education than many. Then a sense of humour and an appreciation of beauty and many other things, for which I can never thank you enough. Anyway, when you love God enough, you can rise above your woes and line up your blessings........ It makes me feel miserable at the thought of you feeling sad about it all. Oh Daddy, we'd be too ungrateful if we didn't think you'd given us all you possibly could and can - please realise it.
Very much love and God bless you Daddy,
Margie P.S. Please could I have some stamps?

After Deirdre married and had her first child Lucy, Margie spent time at Dalmeny House helping her sister. Here's an extract from a letter of August 1957 from Dalmeny House:

"I am moving in horribly high circles and as all my garments are in Griffiths Furniture Store, I am finding it rather difficult and living off Deirdre's wardrobe. We had an iced lobster mousse the other day, it was so delicious, I dribble when I think of it. I eat here for the same reason as the Romans, not because I'm hungry.

Lord Rosebery fell down a hole while grouse shooting yesterday, he shook himself up and is considerably stiff but no serious damage done and his wife has long since recovered from a small bilious attack from some food she ate in someone else's house. Gloves and tiaras may be worn tonight - what shall I wear? Wool mittens and an elastic band?

Margie also wrote letters from France where she stayed with families and taught the children English. Here's part of one from Poissy, near Paris dated January 1959

...yesterday evening for supper, I had a couple of oysters that had been open for two days and some slimy meat and salad. As a result, I spewed frequently throughout the night, my stomach is not yet cast iron like a Frenchman's.

Everyone is progressing with their English - the father now says 'sit down and shut up' to his children at mealtimes and they can all count up to ten and say the verbs to be and to have. Even the four-year-old can say 'a cat'. There are so many typical Frenchmen here - beret, moustache, yellow face etc, that I cannot help laughing...

When the twins started living and working in London, they continued to write to their father, although the letters become rather shorter and to the point:

I shall be able to catch the 4.59 on Friday evening arriving at 6.12. I had an absolutely glorious weekend with Bill and now he is gone, which is very sad. You can laugh Father, and say it puts you in mind of Wodehouse!! I wish, though that I had the wrong kinds of genes and hormones! My boss is still away and won't be back till next week. I think it's the Test Match that makes his bronchitis so bad....

What a lucky man Ronnie was, to have such delightful and very loving children.

Chapter 14

Boring Bit – My Views On Boarding Schools

I walk through the long schoolroom,
- questioning (Yeats)

Much has been written over the years on the merits or drawbacks of boarding schools and there are certainly pros as well as cons. But from my observations, as a boarder for ten years, the pupils who benefited most from the boarding school system were those who came from a secure and loving home where they had been raised in a trauma-free atmosphere – one sufficient to give them a feeling of confidence and security about life in general. In 1948, I was not such a child and boarding school was a huge shock.

Ampleforth 1st XV Rugby, 1959

- Pointless lack of finesse that meant everything was dumbed down and turned into a crowd activity that could be supervised by one person, presumably for cost reasons. Thus, everyone stripped off and showered together, washed together, went to the loo together and slept in huge dormitories with beds close to each other.

- Compulsory religion at very frequent intervals. Roman Catholic doctrine as portrayed in the much-studied Catechism makes grim reading for a child, with its emphasis on original sin, guilt and atonement. And the passion of Christ is a terrifying horror story unless carefully explained.

- Constant negativity in the form of being told you are a bad child, a poor learner or just plain stupid. Children are more sensitive than some teachers appear to think.

I experienced the direct effects of all the above shock factors. They made me feel terrible and they made it virtually impossible for me to connect mentally or emotionally with any of those people running the place. How can you have a civilised conversation with a person who has recently beaten you savagely on your backside? For me, that was not possible, I was too full of hurt pride, rage and feelings of injustice. A small child at preparatory school should not have to deal with that sort of thing.

At the main public school, Ampleforth College, life was more grown up but could still be difficult. Boarding schools by their nature produce a disconnect with one's family and as a result, home life becomes unfamiliar. School holidays are spent partly in trying to rebuild connections with family and friends only to have them disrupted as a new term begins. Such holidays were often boring, my only friends other boarding school children in a similar state.

One such friend was Antony, son of near neighbours, who went to Eton. At the start of each school holiday we would meet up to compare notes. I particularly remember one such time when we were both nearly sixteen. It went like this:

Hello Antony, how was your term?
Not too good I'm afraid
Oh dear, why was that?
Well, my housemaster gave me a really hard time, for no reason.
Oh, that's terrible. What did you do?
I was really pissed off. I got my own back on him though.
Oh? How so?

I seduced his wife.

This conversation was one of the most shocking of my whole childhood, yet my final response was this: My goodness, you Etonians are just so sophisticated. I wish I could be like you!

In actual fact, it later turned out that Ampleforth at the time was probably a lot more nasty and vice-ridden at the time than Eton and several staff were later dismissed for inappropriate behaviour . I just hadn't been aware of what was going on. I think that Ampleforth and schools like it, today struggle to be viable, for a number of reasons. Perhaps it is time for a re-think.

Benedictine monks have never seemed to me particularly suitable people to be involved in running schools of any kind. I think that they would be far better employed tending to the needs of the aged and infirm, as many already do. After all, the ageing population is where the growth lies. There are insufficient facilities for the future increase in numbers of the old and infirm that are predicted. Ampleforth may or may not recover its reputation and thus its economic viability, as a school. But if it does not, here is an alternative business model - it might make a very interesting and well-equipped old people's home.

Chapter 15

My Sisters – Jancis, Lucinda, Caroline

Liquid gold, honeysweet through and through,
Keen-eyed sisters, singing airily,
Looking warily, every way (Tennyson)

There were times as a child, when having three elder sisters seemed like an intolerable burden. Certainly, I was living for most of my pre-teenage years in a home that was predominantly female, and it sometimes hurt. I really longed for a strong male role model or at least a male that I could relate to in some way, someone to confide in. Nevertheless, in many ways they were very kind and loving and I think in retrospect, that over the years I was much more of a burden to them than they were to me.

I actually saw very little of Jancis for the first ten years of my life. She was away at boarding school and even after we had returned to England from India, she spent a lot of her school holidays at our grandfather's house in Camberley – more than the rest of us did.

Jancis had a strong personality, a great sense of humour and was always very supportive of her siblings. She was also extremely clever and after leaving school got a good job at the Foreign Office that she kept until she married, ten years later. This took her to several overseas postings, notably in Germany and Finland.

Jancis, Caroline and Lucinda, 1953

She would write to me at my boarding school - wonderful letters full of her adventures that really lightened my school days. It was while she was in Germany, stationed in Hanover (only a few years after the end of the War) that she met her future husband, David Houston who was then a young British Army officer stationed in Germany. Both of them, through the nature of their jobs, would move around the world over the next ten years but they always kept in touch and anyone could see that they were soulmates.

Jancis and David married in 1959 during my last year at school and I remember the wedding very well. We all stayed at the Savoy Hotel and the wedding was in Chelsea at St Mary's, Cadogan Street and the reception afterwards was at the Savoy, which went on until very late, in the Savoy nightclub. It was all very sophisticated, at least to an eighteen-year-old.

One of the benefits over the year of having a married sister was that I could go and stay with them in the various exotic places where they happened to be stationed. These included Tripoli, various parts of Germany and Washington DC. Since David's regiment was based in Northern Ireland, I also made many trips over there as well.

Jancis and David were always magnificent hosts who put themselves out to give their guests a good time. Consequently, their house was always full of people and entertainment, food and drink always available in abundance. Expeditions happened frequently - a visit to the Berlin Wall, the Hamburg red light district or a day's salmon fishing on the River Shannon. I loved it all.

Jancis and David's two sons Simon and Angus were roughly the same age as our own two boys, which made visits and holidays in later years even more frequent and enjoyable.

David retired from the army, a Major-General, after some very challenging postings in Northern Ireland during the troubles, in recognition of which he was awarded the CBE.

They spent their later years at their lovely house in Sutherland where David was the Lord Lieutenant. The legendary hospitality still flowed freely and continued barely diminished until 2015 when disaster struck one evening, when David had a fall at home and broke his leg very badly. A big heavy man, the local fire brigade had to be called, to carry him downstairs to the ambulance. He never recovered, though the hospital did their best, and he died a few months later. His funeral service at Dornoch Cathedral was very well attended and he was buried at Invershin, beside the Oykel, the great river that he loved to fish.

Just a few weeks later, it became clear that Jancis was gravely ill (we'd all been so concerned about David that we hadn't noticed !) and indeed she died within a very short time and is also buried, beside David, at Invershin. It felt for us all as if a bright light had been switched off for ever.

Lucinda, my second oldest sister, was a leader and reference point in my very early childhood as she and Caroline, my third sister, were with me on our journey from the Far East back to England in 1942. She had, I am glad to say, high moral values and always did what she thought was the right thing and I have a lot to thank her for. I fear that in my twenties, I often abused her hospitality with sometimes drunken and highly inappropriate behaviour, but she never complained and was unfailingly forgiving and kind. Her three children, Joanna, Susan and Richard were always welcoming to our young children too and remain so to this day.

Lucinda married David Gilbert in 1961 – another London wedding and again I walked her down the aisle. David, her husband was a very charming City man, from an old Bermudan family and I would often meet him for lunch, as our offices in the city were near to each other. We would sometimes share a bottle of wine and bemoan our surprising inability to make a fortune in our chosen careers.

For many years they lived at Farnham in Surrey and we spent many happy summer days in the countryside there, sometimes swimming at Frensham Ponds.

Lucinda and David were extremely popular in the neighbourhood and after David retired from the City and they moved to Whitstable, in Kent, they would often return to Farnham to see their old friends and sometimes house-sit for them and look after their pets, when the friends went on holiday.

Sadly, Lucinda too is no longer with us. She died peacefully of heart failure in 2019, after a bravely borne but difficult illness. A merciful end for a very good and sweet person. David currently resides in residential care in Herne Bay, Kent.

My third sister Caroline is just two years older than me and lives in Cumbria. Because we were closest in ages, we played together most when we were very young, though she often preferred to play with her older sister Lucinda, girls together. Sometimes I felt quite isolated.

Burn siblings and spouses, 2002

But my overriding memory of my time with Caroline verges on the horrific: we are both drowning in cold brownish water that seems bottomless. We are sinking and flailing our arms, and slowly rise to the surface to gulp air and again sink beneath that cold, cold water. There is nothing to hold on to, to keep us afloat. My flailing arm reaches Caroline, I cling to her to save myself from sinking, but she kicks me away, a natural reaction of self-preservation. I find her arm again and try to hold on, but we are both going down and she kicks out once again and I am going down, down, down.

I wake up in hospital. We have both been very lucky. During a camping holiday in Wales, Caroline and I were playing in the nearby river estuary and got into difficulty – nobody noticed until too late. Caroline and I have talked about our near-death moment and she has expressed regret at her unfriendly kicks, but she was simply following the instinct of self-preservation.

During my early years in London I would see Caroline regularly when she was living and working there.

Caroline lives in Cumbria now with her Labrador, and little Jack Russell. She has a lot of friends and sees her two children James and Miranda often. James lives nearby at Kingfield, the family home inherited from their father (Caroline and Darrell divorced years ago). Miranda is a highly successful fund manager in the City of London. It is always a pleasure to call in on them when travelling from London to Scotland, as I often do.

Chapter 16

Jolly Japes - What Christopher Did At School

As I learn from you -
I guess you learn from me (Hughes)

It's the school panto and I'm in it. I have to sing a song. I'm dressed in filthy overalls and supposed to be an underground sewer worker. The song is "Down Below":

There is something in a sewer, ... Down below
That has a strange allure, ... Down below,
The magic of the drain, is a thing you can't explain,
But it's calling us again, ... Down below.

It isn't hard to tell .... Down Below,
If it's Bow or Clerkenwell .... Down below
For Bow and Clerkenwell have a different sort of smell,
And we know them very well .... Down below,

It goes on for several verses and the audience loved it. Except for Miss Cornwall, one of our teachers who looked a bit like the Queen would look if she had bad teeth and frizzy hair. And a big bum. Still, the real queen was only about 18 years old then, so you can't know. Anyway, Miss Cornwall didn't like my song. She thought it was nasty and told me so, which spoiled my good feeling. So that night I did a pee outside her room. I thought that was an appropriate gesture, in view of the song's content.

She was furious of course but she couldn't prove anything. She suspected me but I was not saying anything. I was about twelve years old at the time.

I liked the school plays and was in quite a few. Such a Twelfth Night, where I played Sir Toby Belch.

'Twelfth Night', Ampleforth, 1955

I got beaten the year before, for throwing stones at a car. And hitting it. It was a bunch of us, and we hid behind trees by the driveway going up to Gilling Castle, our school. I don't know why we threw stones, it just seemed like a good idea at the time - obviously it was a wrong thing to do but sometimes you just do things anyway. But the man in the car was furious. He stopped and chased us and caught us. He took us straight to the headmaster and demanded that we be punished. Which we were – by six of the best on the bum. It really hurt.

Another time I got beaten was when I was about fourteen. Some of us wanted to go on our bikes to the next little town, called Coxwold. I said the quickest way would be to push our bikes along the railway line as railways don't have steep hills and are usually the shortest distance between two places. So, we went along the railway line which was actually quite stupid and dangerous because a train came along and could have killed us all. So, the train driver made a complaint and when we got back to the school that evening, our housemaster was waiting and it was whack, whack, whack again.

Later in our school days, about the age of sixteen or more, we got much more clever at not getting caught. Our crowd had special places where we could go to smoke, or drink or just hang out, without being found out. We used a sort of code when talking about them, to keep things secret – each place was named after a station on the London Underground – so we'd say for example "we'll meet tomorrow at Piccadilly Circus" which was code for the back room at the Malt Shovel, a local pub, or "Kings Cross" which was Mrs Thompson's house (she would cook us a fry-up and let us smoke) or less attractively, "Hyde Park Corner" which was just an old chicken shed where we could smoke without being seen.

Smoking at that time was an important symbol of rebellion. Smoking was generally not allowed but older boys could smoke at certain special times. Most of the staff and monks smoked anyway. Nobody seemed to bother about the health implications. All quite hypocritical really.

Mr Davidson the history master didn't smoke, and he always smelt beautiful. The finest aftershave. He was a nice man. 'Today we are going to examine the difficulties of Mary Queen of Scots in connection with Queen Elizabeth I of England' he would say. 'And why are you laughing, Burn?' 'It sounds like they are Siamese twins, Sir'. 'Very funny, Burn, now get out of my classroom'. Nice, light-hearted stuff but he gave us the basics of world history that I have never forgotten.

Some people broke the rules far more than I did. A wealthy friend of mine called Colin Crabbe, kept a car in the local village and would go off for jaunts at the weekend. Another boy would slip off to local race meetings whenever he could. I think the headmaster knew, but he must have been a pal or the boy's dad, or else fancied his mother. Or both.

One summer weekend during my last year at school, I and two friends, Gerry Unsworth and George Wardale, invited some girls we knew to come up from London. They stayed at the local hotel and we all went off to Scarborough for a day at the seaside which was blissful and very exciting. This was insanely against the rules, but we didn't care we were leaving school soon anyway. We nearly got caught because we were so late coming back but luckily, nobody noticed. In a school of five hundred boys, it is sometimes surprisingly easy to get away with things.

Once a week, the sixth formers would have a smoking evening where we would all sit around in each other's rooms listening to loud music and smoking ourselves sick. Pretty pointless really, but much better than not sitting around and smoking and listening to loud music.

Social evening, Ampleforth, 1957

All of my last two years at school was in the top end of the sixth form, the 'Scholarship sixth' where we studied exclusively Latin, Greek and Ancient History. We had our own oak-panelled study and thought we were pretty special. We would enjoy discussing the ancient philosophers and amused ourselves with little esoteric rhymes such as:

There was a young curate from Kew
Who kept a Tom Cat in a pew.
He taught it to speak alphabetical Greek
But never got further than μ.

Said the curate "dear pussy you know,
Is that really as far as you go?
If you only would try, you might get up to π
Or even υ or ρ."

It was elegant good fun and as a bit of a change from that sort of thing, I played Rugby too – I was in the school team which was unusual for a Classics scholar. Rugby remains my favourite game to watch though I'm glad that I'm not playing these days, when I see the size and the speed of the players.

Apart from rugby, my school life became more and more focused on the intellectual and cultural side of things.

I am looking now at a book, open in front of me. It is a nicely bound copy of Dr Faustus, Christopher Marlowe's greatest play. There is a short inscription on the first page, in wonderfully ornate Gothic script, written in black ink:

"To Christopher, Christmas Greetings from Michael, December 1958". The Michael in question is Michael Whitehall, who in later life was to become a showbiz agent, a tv personality and the father of comedian Jack Whitehall. This charming present, which I had forgotten for many years, makes me smile because on the page opposite the gracious inscription are stamped the words "Property of Ampleforth College Library".

I came across this book again only recently and I suppose I should return it to its rightful owners. It does illustrate however, the kind of life that my chums and I were leading in the sixth form at Ampleforth. It was a life where an idle but witty gesture was often valued more than moral correctness.

Chapter 17

Accountancy Boot Camp – Mr Anderson's School For Idle Buggers

By swaggering could I never thrive,
For the rain it raineth every day (Shakespeare)

I started my new life as a trainee accountant in London, determined to make a success of myself as a city gent and even bought myself a bowler hat, still in fashion in the fifties.

Although my new firm was very welcoming and not especially demanding, it gradually began to dawn on me that accountancy was not a career that I was well suited to or indeed, even likely to understand properly. My latter years at school had been almost exclusively spent studying the Classics – Latin, Greek and Ancient History with the odd bit of modern history and some French and German lessons thrown in. I had not studied maths much at all and never passed a maths exam in my life.

It came as quite a shock to be expected to add up columns of figures very quickly, but in those days, you had to – there were no computers or electronic calculators to do it for you. As for double entry book-keeping, it took me a long time to fathom what at first seemed a hilariously complicated way of recording money. For me, you either had it or you didn't, and luckily for me, in my youth I did have enough money because following the death of my grandfather, I was left a part of his estate.

However, in the reality of forging a career at Layton-Bennett, Billingham and Co, I was really struggling to do the work needed to qualify as a Chartered Accountant, which involved among other things, the passing of exams.

Ronnie Anderson, Caer Rhun, 1963

I was not the only trainee accountant who found the subject matter difficult and there was indeed a small industry providing private tuition that was designed to meet our needs. The best known of these tuition places was a residential college in North Wales, known as Caer Rhun Hall and it was there that I went after the payment of a fairly substantial fee. It was like going back to boarding school.

Caer Rhun's reputation for success was such that it attracted the majority of the young and fairly idle and rich in the country – people who were wanting the Accountancy qualification but who, frankly, were too busy having a good time with girls and parties and the social scene generally, to be interested or able to devote much or any time to evening studies via correspondence course, which was the way that most people got their knowledge. The idle buggers – I was one of them.

Ronnie Anderson, who founded and ran Caer Rhun, was an accountant extraordinaire. He was always immaculately dressed, travelled by Rolls Royce and smoked cigarettes from a gold case. He was a very witty and charming man and an extremely clever accountant. He was the first of a very small group of accountants that I could respect. In fact, Ronnie inspired me – I wanted to be like him. I think it was that inspiration that got me through the exams successfully – he was a role model that I could aim to imitate.

He would deliver all his lectures and workshops entirely without notes and he never forgot a name or a face. He must have been nearly seventy when I first met him. I ran into him by chance in Malta ten years later and he knew me instantly. A remarkable man indeed.

I first arrived at Caer Rhun in 1960. The car park was full of sports cars and Minis and young men in tweeds were standing about smoking. At the time, there were very few female accountants though thankfully, things began to change quite soon afterwards. We were all allocated rooms that held three or four occupants. It all looked quite jolly. But we were there to work, in fact to be 'crammed' and the process was intensive. Six days a week we did little except get up, take meals and work at lectures and assignments from dawn to dusk. From Saturday lunchtime however, the weekend began, and we really let our hair down. The local Welsh villages and the little seaside towns of Conwy and Colwyn Bay would receive an onslaught of young men determined to get drunk and have a good time.

Here I learned to drink – not as I thought, like a man, but like a fish. It was I suppose, a form of release but it ended up being a goal and indeed, even an obsession.

Everyone else seemed to be doing the same but that was no real excuse. I don't know how our battered brains coped with it all, but somehow, we survived this weird accountants' boot camp and most of us, myself included, passed our exams as a result. I went to Caer Rhun three times during my training and it became almost as familiar as my old school. And I made some good friends there too, including Michael Houghton concerning whom there is nothing dull, and Norman Spiteri, whom I later teamed up with in Malta.

Back in London, I continued with my accountancy and determined to get the Chartered Accountants qualification come what may, although I was becoming increasingly disillusioned with it all. I could see however, that it gave one a good income and after all, I didn't have an alternative.

There were some nice people at Layton-Bennett's including my lifelong friend from then on – Peter Lindsay who joined the firm a year after me and amazingly to me, managed to qualify, through dint of sheer hard work and evening study – something that I had not been capable of.

Chapter 18

Dodo – Granny Wynne-Roberts

Seldom I mark mankind's detested ways,
Not hearing censure or affecting praise (Montagu)

During my first few years in London, I had shared lodgings in Earls Court with an old school friend, George Wardale. George and I were both training to be Chartered Accountants and had a lot in common. On weekends, he would often invite me to his family home in Berkshire, because Yorkshire was too far and too expensive for a weekend. His mother Betty, and younger sister, Beverley were always very hospitable, and I really enjoyed their company.

Often on Saturday evenings we would all go over to dinner to his grandmother, Mrs Dorothy Wynn Roberts, known to her friends as Dodo (though to us youngsters she was known simply as 'Granny'.) Quite soon, I started going out with Beverley, a sweet and very entertaining girl, who had left school and started a secretarial course in London. I now had an extra reason for my weekend visits and Beverley and I would often make the short trip down to Wokingham.

Dodo lived in a beautiful large old house at Wokingham set in a big garden with a lovely grass tennis court that we used a lot. A cigarette butt constantly between her lips, she would totter round the house and garden shouting at the gardener, the daily help and her guests as well, though in the nicest possible manner. She saw it as part of her mission to bring up George as a gentleman since his father had vanished to New Zealand following a divorce. This involved shouting at him too. George resisted this attention and generally acted badly, becoming rude and resentful, but that didn't bother Dodo, whose ancestry (she was a Napier) went back to several Generals who had helped to conquer India in the eighteenth century. Taming George was a relatively minor campaign for her, even though she was at quite an advanced age.

The house was full of wonderful furniture and paintings and she had lived many years of married life on a tea plantation in Ceylon. A very forthright person with a strong sense of right and wrong, she could be very argumentative though also very realistic. She and her husband would travel everywhere in separate cars, even for short trips, because they were so prone to arguing. It was probably a very sensible arrangement that perhaps others might try. Sadly, her husband pre-deceased her by many years.

Ireland, 1964

Dodo loved dining out or just going to the local pubs where she and her beautiful Border Collie, Timothy were well known. Timothy was the original reason why I eventually ended up with Bonnie, my very own Collie, years later. They were almost identical.

One year, we all went off on a holiday to West Cork, in Ireland, which was bliss.

I'd been to Ireland before but not quite like this. The tiny village of Schull was little known in those days and the East End Hotel, where we stayed for two weeks, was its social hub. It seemed as if every person who came into the bar was a character recognisable from every Irish book, play or film you'd ever come across – the Tinker, the Drinker, the Traveller, The Fisherman, the Racing Man, the Priest, the Horse Dealer and of course The Playboy of the Western World, oozing romantic charm from every pore. I had never drunk Guinness before but an evening in the company of the two local gravediggers put me right. Every night the singing would start and continue into the early hours. I thought it was magical on that first trip and I couldn't get enough of it. A loveable but wily merchant called John Goggin sold me a derelict cottage with a tiny strip of land one night for two hundred pounds and I thought that I had bought a piece of heaven. I wanted to live there for ever and drink and sing in the bar of the East End Hotel until I died.

Dodo and Betty and Beverley loved it too. One day we took a trip into Dodo's past – to see the ruins of a great house of distant relations, where she had holidayed in Edwardian times, before it had been burnt down during the struggle for Irish Independence. It was a reminder that we were in the heartland of Irish nationalism, where many deadly incidents had taken place in years gone by.

Our Irish party-time came to an end and it was back to accounting in the City of London and the daily grind. But I was now an Irish landowner and made more visits in the following years. Gradually though, I fell out of love with the place. I'm not quite sure why. Perhaps it was giving me too many hangovers. Probably it was a feeling of unease that grew as the troubles and the ill feelings around Irish nationalism reappeared.

It's one thing to be singing romantic love songs in a Irish bar, it's quite another to be surrounded by people singing rebel songs who are glorifying the killing of English people and looking at you with hate in their eyes. It made me so uneasy in fact, that after a few years, I sold my little piece of heaven and never went back.

But I kept going back to see Dodo. She was unfailingly hospitable even after I moved abroad, married and accordingly visited less frequently.

Dodo continued living in her lovely house and gardens until the day she died. She had lived there alone for much of the time, but this didn't seem to worry her. I was away working in Paris at the time and it was a sad day when I heard the news.

She died peacefully in her bed one night. I think she must have been well over ninety years old, but she had full command of her faculties. A truly remarkable and memorable lady and a fine role model, she was afraid of nothing and nobody. In her bed they also found her diamonds, a bottle of whisky and a loaded revolver. She liked to be well prepared for any eventuality.

Chapter 19

A Car Crash – Cromwell Road, London

The motor car went Poop, Poop, Poop
As it raced along the road (Carroll)

It is a rather nice evening in June, and I am driving down the Cromwell road, an important traffic artery in West London. My new Mini is purring along nicely. I haven't had it very long, it was a 21st birthday present to myself and I love it. It is pale blue with lots of shiny chromium bits. I've added a few extra things – a second exhaust pipe, a spotlight on the roof, and a touch of black and white chequered tape across the bonnet. Nothing too flashy but the effect is really special. And this car can move. They tweaked the engine a bit so I can get away from the lights like a rocket. And at this time of night the traffic is moving quite fast.

I'm on my way back from the pub, The Anglesea in Onslow Gardens. We've been on pints of bitter, quite a few actually, but I'm feeling really good and wondering if I'll get to the Scarsdale Arms in time for a quick one before they close. It's good that the traffic's not heavy, so I can hurry.

At this time of night there are cars parked along the side of the road to my left but there's still plenty of room. It's dark but there are lots of street-lights and I'm not worried. Then this Porsche suddenly backs out from the parked cars on the left and I haven't time to avoid him. I'm going too fast. Maybe my reactions are slow. My front wing hits the back corner of the Porsche and the little Mini spins sideways and flips over onto its roof. There are dreadful sounds of rending metal, breaking glass and wailing horns. Then silence.

I am upside down in the Mini and I can't get out. A crowd gathers and the police quickly arrive. I am confused, disoriented and shaking. I realise I am also slightly drunk. Weirdly, everyone including the police, are terribly kind and helpful. They think I am in shock and they put a blanket round me. A truck comes and drags my broken little Mini away. The Porsche owner turns out to be from the German embassy - the Cultural Attache. He is very kind, and cultural, and offers help. Then the police offer to take me home in their car and tell me to go to bed with a hot drink.

Nobody mentions drink driving. Nobody threatens prosecution. It is years before breathalysers were introduced. I wake the next morning with a bad hangover. The car is a write-off.

What I should have learned:

-Never ever drink and drive
-Don't expect to get away with things ever again
-Change your driving attitude, it will get you into trouble.

Instead, I carried on just as before, storing up trouble, inevitably, for the future.

Chapter 20

Friends In Flats – London Life

Controls them and subdues, transmutes, bereaves,
Of their bad influence, and their good receives (Wordsworth)

Coming to live in London straight from a boys-only public school was always going to cause a few problems. Sharing a flat with some of my school pals was not a terribly good idea either. We simply weren't civilised. None of us had any idea or any inclination towards housework, washing, cooking or simple tidiness, with the result that we were soon living in a midden. Floors were never swept, bed linen never changed, rubbish seldom thrown out. On top of that, every now and then we would throw a party. This would not be a sophisticated affair, just a bring your own bottle do. I don't think we even provided glasses. These could quickly get out of hand and deteriorate into some pretty anti-social behaviour and the neighbours would complain loud and long. I remember coming back to our flat in Nevern Square after a weekend in Yorkshire to find that there had been a party in my absence and my bed had been thrown out of the window and was now on the pavement (it was a third floor flat). We were not nice people to live near.

Living in a shared flat was cheap, which was good for me – as an 'Articled Clerk' studying Accountancy, I was a kind of student working an office routine but paid student rates – I started at £3 per week. The flat was not however, a good place to do homework, of the kind that I was expected to do most evenings. Soon I simply gave up and went to the pub like everyone else. I did manage to pass my accountancy exams by going to a special school in Wales (the Boot Camp described elsewhere). This got me the qualification of Chartered Accountant that I needed, but I still didn't really understand enough about the profession I had so unwisely decided to join.

Beverley, John, Patrick, Mike, Me, 1963

All that didn't seem to matter in the early days. It seemed much more important to be going to the right parties and social events with the right people. We may have been ignorant and uncivilised in those days, but we all had connections of some kind or other with smart society. Our expensive schooling had at least given us that. Somehow, we would emerge from time to time, out of our dreadful rubbish tip of a flat all dressed up to the nines for Royal Ascot, or in immaculate evening dress to attend a dinner dance in Park Lane. If our hostesses had only known, they would not have let their daughters anywhere near us.

One of my flatmates – John Bracey, was convicted of perjury in a drink driving case and had to leave for Australia in a hurry. Nobody seemed particularly surprised or indeed judgemental, though John's mother living in respectable Surbiton, got a nasty shock when she opened the morning paper to see the headline 'Local Man Told Pack of Lies' above a photo of her son. In fact, she cut him out of the inheritance. When I last heard, twenty years ago, John was still in Australia.

Patrick Robinson, a journalist at the Daily Express, was another flatmate. He was later, to go to America and became a best-selling author. He worked on the Sports page at the Express and always had press tickets for big events such as Wimbledon, the Derby or The Open Golf tournament. Going to some of these places with him, I met lots of famous sportsmen of the time – Rod Laver, Billie-Jean King, Lester Pigott and my particular golfing hero, Arnold Palmer. Patrick and I used to do a lot of drinking too. In fact, looking back on it all, I don't know how I found the time to go to work in the City. I think my employers, the Accountants Layton-Bennett, Billingham must have taken a dim view of my performance, but they didn't say much.

After a bad car crash and several years of this sort of life, I think I grew up a bit. My sister Caroline offered me a bedsit in the basement of her large house in Kensington and I jumped at it.

Here, life was a bit more normal and regulated and I was able to actually do some work and some studying though by now, at age of 21, I had definitely acquired a taste for alcohol. In terms of priority, my list read:

Alcohol, Parties, Sport, Girls, Work.

My idea of a good evening would be squash at the Hurlingham club with a friend followed by a meal and lots of beer. Or sometimes Antony Lawson Smith, or Gilbert Thompson-Royds, my old friends from Yorkshire would come round and we would play cards and share a bottle of whisky.

Caroline and her husband Darrell were very good to me and often fed me. Sometimes I would go up to Cumbria with them for a long weekend at Kingfield, Darrell's family home that he had recently inherited, where we would do some shooting and walking.

I thought at the time that I was living the life of a successful man about town, working hard and playing hard, but this was an illusion. In reality I was hanging on by my fingertips. My attitude to life was extremely immature – I was doing the things I liked and running away from those I didn't like. And alcohol was becoming my crutch. It was even starting to make me ill.

Caroline and Darrell sold their London House in 1963 and I had to move. I found a nice little flat in Grosvenor Crescent Mews, between Belgrave Square and Hyde Park Corner and moved in. I was now on my own, my flat-sharing days behind me, and I loved it.

The mews house had two flats and the other was occupied by Christine Keeler. Her name does not resonate so much nowadays but in 1964 it was huge. Christine had been at the centre of a scandal that rocked the government and caused the resignation of John Profumo, a Cabinet Minister who lied to

Parliament in denying that he had had a relationship with Keeler. The papers had been full of it.

Poor Christine received a pasting at the hands of the press and by the time that I met her, she was thoroughly fed up with the whole thing. That didn't stop her having some riotous parties and some of her friends were actually quite unpleasant. The walls between the two flats were thin and I occasionally heard more than I wanted to. One night I was woken by her shouting 'Get out of my bed, all three of you!' She was quite apologetic in the morning. I liked Christine, basically she was a nice simple girl who had got into something she wasn't expecting and couldn't handle. And she was very beautiful.

Chapter 21

Workplace Adventures – London Labours

What are we set on earth for? Say, to toil –
Nor seek to leave thy tending of the vines (Barrett Browning)

I became a Chartered Accountant. How and why are mysteries I still have not answered. The process took me five years to achieve. As an articled clerk, I was part of a team of auditors who travelled from business to business examining their finances and certifying the accuracy of their accounts. It sounds quite boring and most of the time, it was. An American colleague described it as "looking up a dead horse's ass.* I could sort of see what he meant.

The clients that we visited in this way were a varied lot: banks, newspapers, chicken farmers, printers, hotels, paper makers and gentlemen's clubs were just a few. I enjoyed travelling and saw many parts of the country and many businesses that I might otherwise never have known about. A wine importer in Exeter and a small book publisher in Kent I still think of as delightful businesses to visit and ones that must have been a pleasure to operate as well.

As I gained in experience, I would sometimes visit clients alone. We had a client in Bournemouth and I would drive there early in the morning sometimes with Beverley in the car too – I would leave her on the beach until I'd finished work then motor back to town, stopping for dinner on the way.

George Wardale, my old school chum, was working in another accountancy firm, though he took it all more seriously than I did. I think he thought my approach was much too frivolous and he was probably right. Years later, he was a very high-powered financial consultant while I was basically struggling. I was to admire his skills but then, I called him a swot.

One client that I secretly admired was in the City of London and was known as a discount house. Basically, they moved huge sums of money round the bond market and the banks, taking advantage of fluctuations in interest rates. It was all very gentlemanly, and they wore beautiful Savile Row suits and smoked big cigars and had a private dining room for long lunches where fine wines were consumed. Awesome. I opened an account at Coutts and Co, then London's smartest bankers and bought a new suit and pretended I was like them, but it fooled nobody.

Peter Lindsay and I started a little investment company of our own called Hopefully [illegible] Ltd but we didn't really know what we were doing.

What I really wanted, as I now see, were the results of a successful City career – the clothes, the money, the lunches - without being prepared to do the necessary hard work. –All very immature and, I'm afraid, a recipe for failure. I was trying to be something I was not cut out to be and it was causing me unnecessary stress.

Then disaster struck. Soon after I had taken my final exams, I went out to dinner with friends to celebrate, though not yet knowing the results. At dinner, I ordered an Italian wine called 'Lacrima Christi' (the tears of Christ) that comes from the slopes of Mount Vesuvius. It is a good white wine though rather acidic. The next morning, I woke up feeling very ill indeed. At first I put it down to the customary hangover but I was wrong. I had a perforated duodenal ulcer and had lost a lot of blood. Luckily for me, Beverley called round by chance and found me too ill to move. But with her help, I managed to walk the few yards to St George's Hospital which was almost next door to my flat. Here I was rushed to A and E, given several pints of blood and then operated on and the ulcer repaired. I spent a week in St George's being pampered by sweet student nurses, night and day. I didn't want to leave when the time came. The NHS was different then. But leave I did, with great gratitude. I had been lucky to survive.

This incident was a strong warning sign. Very few 24-year-olds get perforated ulcers. At that age, they are usually the sign of a very dissipated lifestyle as indeed mine was. I had been taking in far too much alcohol, eating unhealthily and taking very little exercise. The warning bells had sounded but I was not listening

I remember the doctor telling me not to drink alcohol. I agreed, but I was back drinking within a couple of weeks. And now I seemed to be drinking more. It was as if I had a new stomach, one specially designed for the purposes of drinking. The next month I got drunk at the firm's annual dinner and insulted the senior partner. I began to feel that a change was needed. It was time to move on.

By chance, another school friend, Leo Cavendish, had just returned from Paris and was telling me all about it. The atmosphere, the fun, the wine that flowed all day… I started making enquiries about work. Sure enough, there were lots of accountancy firms recruiting for their Paris office and I was offered a job at the first interview. I took it without hesitating.

I wrote a letter to my old firm, Layton Bennett, Billingham & Co who had put up with my obnoxious attitude and tiresome behaviour for almost six years. I apologised for the short notice. It was a great opportunity I said, to further my career, and I needed to make the change as soon as possible.

They replied by return saying that they quite agreed there was a need for change and that I could therefore leave immediately. I was too naïve and too stupid to see what they were really saying.

Chapter 22

The Muse In The Mews – Margie's Poems

So long as men can breathe or eyes can see,
So long lives this, and this gives life to thee (Shakespeare)

As I left the house, I was smitten by a teddy bear. It bounced off my head onto the dusty cobblestones. I couldn't just leave it lying there gazing up at the summer stars - who knows what might happen to an abandoned teddy bear, even in a smart Kensington Mews. So, I went back inside and upstairs to her bedroom. A room that she chastely shared with another girl, though tonight she was alone. I didn't stay long. But long enough to kindle something. Not that anything actually happened – this was 1964 and although the 'pill' had been recently invented, most girls hadn't really got into the swing of things then, not like they did a little later on.

So that's how it started. There was never a dull moment with Margie. Whenever things were winding down, a teddy bear would come out of nowhere to hit you.

We had so much in common - dining and going to pubs and theatres and galleries and clubs. And we were both going to Paris to work. And we shared the same sense of humour. And we liked new ideas and poetry and creativity. Or just chatting about nothing much. But always delivered with wit – as was her poetry, such as this, a reaction to the 'over-erudite' modern poets such as TS Eliot and Ezra Pound:

Though Eliot Pounded, his voice could soar;
A sufficient reason to feel less drenched

Is "Here the crow starves" from "Rannoch Moor".
I forgive his three poems in perfect French
And admire the humble taking of stock,
In "The Love Song of J Alfred Prufrock".

(Her hand-written note beside this, reads: Shame I didn't send this to a poetry magazine at the time. I might have met some like-minded people, e.g. bearded gits in sandals.)

The two years we spent in Paris were the most bittersweet experience. So much that was new but so many faux pas by me in so many ways. I know I made her unhappy at times, right from the start, but somehow, we made it through. We learnt a lot and stressed a lot and loved a lot. And as spring came around, she wrote this happy poem from her desk at UNESCO:

Tear up the red tape, the letters and passes,
To weave into garlands and bind in your hair.
Let's make a maypole of concrete and chromium
Festooned with shorthand to stream in the air.
We'll dance to the music of typewriters thrashing,
Of telephones ringing and no-one to care.
Death to the fetish of civil servility,
Death to the boredom of eight hours a day.
We'll burst out of bondage like stars from a rocket,
The will of Jehovah! So, let it be May.

I think that Margie turned to poetry for fun mostly, but sometimes to relieve boredom too. Or just to help express herself in more interesting ways. In 1981, our marriage was going through a very rocky time indeed, entirely due to my excessive drinking and consequent bad behaviour. I had already been to rehab without success. Britain itself was in quite a mess too. There were riots and economic problems. Margie's response was to write this poem on the economic situation, which she sent to the Financial Times:

Inflation decreasing the size of loans
So capital debts look mere bagatelles,
And banking circles resound with the groans
Of those whose capital shrivels pell mell.
So spenders and lenders can plainly see

That their interests diverge or fluctuate
As post-Keynesian pundits can't agree
If it's right to let the markets dictate.

But high bank charges make firms go under
So, bang goes all profit in wheeling and dealing
When venture capital comes asunder,
As interest rates hit the boardroom ceiling.
The maxim's upended – it's come to pass
That banking generates muck from brass.

Her note on this poem says: This one received a personal note from the deputy editor of the FT, saying how he'd liked it, but they didn't publish poetry, but try the Observer – which I didn't

Even when the children were small and requiring a lot of attention, Margie was always trying to do part time secretarial work whenever she could. It was desperately tiring for her, but she was nothing if not resilient. And always cheerful. Sometimes her temporary work took her into the heart of the City of London, a place that sometimes horrified her because of the sheer drudgery of the type of work that she was called upon to do. Here is one response in four short lines:

They're sightless with excitement
As they bustle down the Drain.
It's two minutes past monotony
And mankind must catch his train.

As the slow car crash of our married life progressed, life became extremely stressful for Margie. Not surprisingly, her poetry-writing seems to have dried up at around this time though her letter-writing and her conversation continued to be as poetic as ever.

I had always supposed that Margie started writing poetry in her twenties, but I recently found a poem that is dated New Hall, 1956 – when she was sixteen years old. It is surprisingly thoughtful and profound for one so young. I also think it is quite beautiful and comforting and I would love to think that she remembers it now. Indeed, I will show it to her when I get the chance.

The Consoler

Oh, Why did he go?
Why did he not stay?
Why did he suddenly fly away?
Just when I needed him most.

I do not know,
But I have heard say
That, in grief, he has to fly.
He goes far away when his loved ones die.
He weeps for his loss throughout the night,
But he will be back with a wind so light
When he has mourned enough.
He will not let your spirit break,
He tempered your soul,
He knows.
So, go to your door at the break of dawn
And watch your consoler wing in on the morn.

Later on, it was me who started writing and publishing, drawing sometimes on her example. She was my inspiration. Whatever I write, at the back of my mind is the thought "what would Margie think of this?" My Muse in the Mews.

Chapter 23

Danse Difficile - Margie And Work

The apparition of these faces in a crowd;
Petals on a wet, black bough (Pound)

By the start of 1965, I was in need of change. I had been working at the same job in the same firm all that time and had somehow managed to qualify as a Chartered Accountant, although I disliked the whole concept of accountancy and auditing. I was not a natural numbers person, having never passed or indeed taken a maths exam. Stuff like algebra and calculus were a foreign country to me.

In my classical studies I had read (as who has not?) the wonderful work by Professor EH Kitto, 'The Greeks' and had come across this passage where he talks about the amazing discoveries made by the likes of Pythagoras and Euclid, who worked out mathematical and geometric theorems, with little more than sand and a stick to draw with. I could sort of see what he meant by the beauty of the dance of numbers:

"They had never told me, and I had never suspected, that Numbers play these grave and beautiful games with each other, from everlasting to everlasting, independently (apparently) of time, space and the human mind. "

But I couldn't understand how they worked. This needed to change.

Indeed, change was in the air, but I failed to realise that it was me and my 'couldn't care less' and immature 'I want my cake and eat it' personality, that needed to change. I had different ideas.

I decided that a geographical change would sort out all my problems, and I went for a job interview to join leading accountants Price Waterhouse & Co, in Paris. I was offered the job and accepted, starting in a month's time.

Arriving alone in Paris was a huge culture shock and I felt insecure and anxious. My French was pretty rudimentary and though I went to evening classes, it took time to improve and simply added to my anxieties.

My first night, I stayed at the Hotel de Calais near Place Vendôme and in the morning walked round to Avenue de l'Opera, where Price Waterhouse was situated. It was all very strange, and I was extremely nervous. I met a whole lot of new people – Partners, Accountants and Secretaries who were all extremely nice and helpful and I began to realise the enormity of the changes that I had set in motion. I was having to adapt to a new job (in a profession I didn't like and didn't really understand), in a new language. In addition, I had to find new friends and somewhere to live, in a totally strange city.

On my first day I was told that I would be going in 'at the deep end'. By this they meant that I was to travel immediately to Dijon, a town several hours journey from Paris, where I was to supervise a stocktake at the Hoover Washing Machine factory. It meant a two-night stay in Dijon. My anxiety levels went through the roof, but that evening found me on the train.

At the factory the next morning, there were nice guys and not so nice guys too, but no one who would admit to speaking English. In 1965, English did not have the almost global coverage as a lingua franca that it does today. The French in particular, were very protective of their mother tongue.

When you are checking a stock of washing machine parts in a foreign language of which you have only limited grasp, it is going to be difficult. Many parts have unfathomable names, even in English. Somehow, we got through. The chief financial officer took me out to dinner that night. He took his mistress along too. We had snails and boeuf à la Bourguignonne. It was all as French as any experience could get.

After Dijon, Paris seemed bearable and it got better. Margie came out to work and lived with some friends in Rue la Condamine - très bohème, while I found a tiny flat by the Étoile – très chic. Soon she came to live with me.

Margie in Paris, 1965

The flat was charming and tiny and again, very French. By that I mean that it had a concierge, a delightful garden and very, very dodgy plumbing. So dodgy in fact that the kitchen and bathroom were combined in one room. Never a good plan, it caused numerous problems which we always somehow overcame without drowning, electrocuting or infecting ourselves.

Dammit, we were together in Paris, we were young, and we were in love. I have never experienced such an intensely emotional time as then. Years later, when I read Ernest Hemingway's famous words about Paris, I knew exactly what he meant: "If you are lucky enough to have lived in Paris as a young man, then wherever you go for the rest of your life, it stays with you, for Paris is a moveable feast." It's a cliché, but it's true.

Chapter 24

La Vie En Rose – Paris, Margie And Marriage

Des mots de tous les jours
Et ça m'fait quelque chose (Piaf - song)

Paris in the 1960's had opportunities for enjoyment and culture that were light years ahead of the UK. Margie and I took advantage of most of them. Most obvious of course was the food. At a time when London restaurants were, with extremely few exceptions, very mediocre, Paris was bursting with family run bistros, brasseries and cordon bleu restaurants. Within yards of our little flat, there were at least six small eateries serving beautiful food, very reasonably priced. In addition, there were also street oyster vendors, butchers, bakers and delicatessens where exquisite ingredients could be found, any day of the week. There was really no need to cook at all, perhaps fortuitously, given the fact that our kitchen was also our loo!

Prue and Gordon came to visit one weekend in May, and we spent an evening on one of the magnificent bateaux mouches – the large pleasure boats that glided up and down the Seine (and still do), giving superb views of floodlit Notre Dame, the Sainte Chapelle and the Eiffel Tower while serving top class dinners and lunches. London had nothing comparable at the time.

With Prue & Gordon, Bateau Mouche, 1965

Other weekends we would go racing at Longchamp or Auteuil, the two tracks in the Bois de Boulogne on the West side of the city. Here, the chic demeanour of the racegoers and the gracious buildings produced an experience memorable for its elegance and class. Longchamp is still one of my favourite places.

But such outings had their dangers. I remember walking home after the races and a gutsy dinner with Margie and some friends in the super-smart eighth arrondissement. Snails, coq au vin and crèpes had been liberally consumed plus lots of red wine. Unfortunately, just as we passed the entrance of the luxurious George V Hotel, Margie was overcome and threw up her dinner on their red carpet and some of their arriving guests too! The terrifying portier d'hotel (doorman) had some very choice things to say although since he was a Frenchman addressing a pretty young lady, I had to admire his relative restraint, even gallantry.

Weirdly, when I was in Scotland years later, I met a man at a dinner party who said he had been the doorman at the George V. When I told him the story, he said he remembered the incident!

There was something very exciting about being English and in France, at that time. It was only ten years since the end of World War II and I suppose the rest of Europe viewed us in a pretty good light, especially the French since we had helped de Gaulle, the Free French and of course the Resistance so much.

It was also a good time to be working as an accountant in France. Business was booming there, largely because US companies were starting to expand into Europe in a big way, often by buying up French companies in similar lines of business – motor, electric goods and foodstuffs especially. This meant a lot of work for us and the firm of Price Waterhouse, with its massive US client base, did very well indeed. We, the foot-soldiers, were treated very well. First class travel was considered part of the image and the basic pay was pretty good too. It was a great way to see the country. I became used to spending time in smart hotels and dining on expense account meals, sometimes perhaps too well.

In May 1966 Margie and I decided to get married and the wedding was set for the end of July, in London. It was all very exciting. Margie went back to London to organise things and I travelled back a week before the wedding was due. There were stag parties, hen parties and all the usual wedding hassle. I must say that I found it all quite difficult to handle, even though I was lucky enough not to have to do much of the organising. I think I knew that I was an introvert, and quite a sociophobic one too, though I didn't admit it to myself. I relied on alcohol to 'loosen up and relax' myself, and this was not a good thing. I was starting to rely on it as a social crutch.

Wedding day came and I was in a high state of nervousness. I gathered my 'team' in the morning – best man David Armitage, and ushers Andrew Brand, Duncan Brand, Antony Lawson-Smith, Patrick Robinson, David Reid. We had a few glasses of champagne before going to the church – not a good idea in retrospect. I was certainly in good form when we got to the church, perhaps too good form. Fr Oswald Vanheems, the Ampleforth monk who had been my housemaster, was there to perform the service. That sobered me up a bit. I hadn't seen him since school days and he still had that slightly disapproving air.

The ceremony went well with beautiful singing in a packed church. I was in a bit of a daze already. Back to Crosby Hall, on the Embankment for the reception, and more champagne. Oh dear, I was starting to lose the plot. I made a speech of thanks and kept it pretty short. I could tell that it should have been longer and more effusive, but I didn't trust myself. It was not done well, but at least it was done. There were other distractions too – it was the day of the World Cup final, and England were playing Germany. The match was on at the time of my speech, and a lot of people were more focused on the football than on me. And soon the news was out – England had won the World Cup! It seemed that the whole country was suddenly in celebration mode and getting quite drunk – just like me.

Wedding Day, 30th July, 1966

Later on, Margie and I left the reception in the traditional way and spent the night at the Compleat Angler in Marlowe, a lovely hotel in the Thames valley, before returning to France for our honeymoon.

Chapter 25

Itchy Feet - Camden, The Caribbean And The Med

Yet all experience is an arch wherethrough
Gleams that untraveled world (Tennyson)

Margie and I returned to London in late 1967 after nearly two years in Paris. Swinging London was a great place to be and we found a little house in Camden Town, then a quite unfashionable place to live but it suited us well. Our friends Tim and Amelia Fell lived nearby and there was an easy-going ambience about the place. I was offered a job through a family connection, with John Bidwell and David Gough, both young financiers who were trying to exploit the freewheeling times and exciting new opportunities that were around as the world slowly recovered from the devastation of two World Wars.

Their company, Arlington Securities, had large interests in the Bahamas, especially property development. Air travel was expanding hugely and the American market for property in the sun was huge. We would take potential investors out to Grand Bahama Island, give them a good time and hopefully sell them some choice real estate.

It didn't always work out, but it was a fun business to be in with lots of colourful characters. We operated out of a small regency town house in Belgravia opposite one owned by our business rival and more successful property developer, the Hon Colin Tennant who was busily developing Mustique.

I flew out on one occasion via New York and felt for the first time the excitement of going to exotic places. That excitement has never left me. On that first trip to the Caribbean, I was totally unprepared for the life of the Caribbean. I got off the plane at Grand Bahama Island still dressed like a London City gent in a shirt and tie and three-piece suit. How the locals laughed as I melted in the heat and humidity.

It didn't take long to get into the swing of things and enjoy the poolside lifestyle. The Bahamas are just a hop by plane from Miami and very popular with the Americans. Such a culture change from 1960's Britain, I have never forgotten the shock.

However, partly due to the proximity of Miami and organised crime, the Bahamas soon acquired a negative reputation, and our London operation ran into trouble. The staff and directors gathered for one last monumental blast at the local pub (Black Velvet flowing freely) and then it was all over. John and David went off to more conventional stockbroking positions in the City. I had other plans afoot.

During my years training as an accountant, I had met, while at Mr Anderson's accountancy cramming establishment, a young Maltese chap called Norman Spiteri. Norman had been educated in the UK and was an ambitious go-getter. After qualifying a couple of years previously, he had set up in practice in Malta as a professional accountant and things were going well. He was looking for a partner to help expand the business and approached me. It came at just the right time, as the Bahamas project was failing, and I was interested.

Looking back, I can see that what I was really after was something that would rescue me from what I saw as the appalling drudgery of a typical accountant's life in the UK – endless repetition, number crunching, boring routine production of financial results, no outlet for creativity of any kind. To my rather immature mind, this was akin to a life sentence in an open prison. Norman was offering something a bit different, where I could be involved in running the show and indulge in some entrepreneurial activity as well (though I wasn't even sure quite what that meant yet).

Margie, Johnnie, Alex, Harry Dalmeny, Malta 1971

Margie wasn't very keen – and who could blame her – young Alexander, our first child, was only one year old and she was reluctant to leave the support of her family and friends in London to embark on a jaunt to an unknown island in the Mediterranean.

By chance, Prue and Gordon had recently bought a property in Malta and were embarking on the retired expat life (with tax breaks) at this same time. Margie and I went out to Malta for a holiday with them in their nice house in Naxxar and that helped us to decide.

The upshot was that in early 1969, I flew out to Malta to start work with Norman and Margie and Alexander followed soon after. It was not easy at first – Malta was only just starting to become a viable tourist destination and though there were many fledgling businesses, the general impression was of an island that was in many ways living still in the pre-World War II era ! British forces were still very much in residence in many army barracks and also, in the huge naval dockyard at Valletta.

However, it was a very friendly and pro-British place overall, and everyone spoke English. The climate was exceptional and it was a great place to bring up small children. As we got used to the place, we began to really enjoy our time there. Our second son Johnnie was born in Malta, at the British Naval Hospital in Mtarfa.

There were some truly lovely friends that we made or renewed there – John and

Bride Hill, parents of Andrew Brand's wife Thea, had lived there several years – John taught at the University. They were the nicest and kindest of people whose hospitality knew no bounds and they introduced us to scores of other people. John took me on a tour of Valletta and introduced me to his tailor, his shoemaker, and his shirtmaker, all ridiculously cheap for the excellent work they produced. Without the Hills, our life in Malta would have been a lot less enjoyable.

This little island became a very pleasant home to us for four years and it was really sad that we eventually had to leave. Seeing Maltese Independence happen - the British turfed out of the dockyard and us having to follow, due to a change of government (and general mood) in Malta, was living through a little piece of history. But at the time it felt extremely painful.

Chapter 26

A Haven For Black Sheep - Malta People

And I have asked to be
Where no storms come (Hopkins)

One of the attractions of Malta in the late 1960s was its function as a haven, perhaps even a magnet, for black sheep from all over the world. Mostly these were of a minor nature and included expats with a past, visiting businessmen with dodgy agendas, yacht-based buccaneers, fugitive politicians and a few local wannabe plutocrats. The word that came to mind was pirates.

As accountants, our offices were a popular point of call for a lot of such people who were usually after information on the local tax arrangements, sources of finance (especially those with not too rigorous lending criteria), potential business partners, property deals or even just an introduction to the best of the local nightlife. I was always happy to oblige, especially as such conversations often involved a visit to a local bar or a boozy lunch.

Tony Robinson was an example. He simply breezed into our office one morning carrying a black briefcase (which I was to discover later, contained a bottle of whisky and not much else). Tony had a successful UK business providing background music to supermarkets and wanted to mitigate UK tax by transferring profits to Malta (then a low-tax country). He had already devised a clever way of doing this, which I had better not divulge, and simply wanted us to run the operation through a local company. It was all simple, legal and easily arranged. What he also wanted, like many others, was a few days away from his wife and family having a good time.

A man in his fifties, he was tall, slightly overweight with longish silvery hair that curled over the back of his collar. He had a hook nose, reddened by drink, a moustache, and a loud laugh. He looked and acted like a pirate, and that was what he was.

I took him to lunch and that lasted till the evening. He was the sort of client that I really responded to. Always on the lookout for a quick deal, he got involved in the Malta property market and did well. He was also a keen yachtsman and would charter boats rather than owning them himself.

The Marinas in Malta were full of desirable floating gin palaces with idle skippers on board, longing to do some charter work. We quickly identified a suitable craft, skippered by one of the yachting legends of the time – Monty Lewis.

Dishonest, materialistic and alcoholic, Monty was also reckoned to be the best skipper in the Med and when sober, he probably was. He had certainly sailed all over the world in small boats and had a huge understanding of his profession. He was a raconteur without match who liked nothing better than to hold forth in a pub while consuming huge amounts of alcohol. His wife and children who lived with him in a small flat in Malta, suffered greatly from his behaviour and the inevitable divorce happened. Monty was an undoubted rogue but a very amusing one, provided you were not one of his victims.

The combination of these two buccaneers was entertaining but highly dangerous. Though they provided me with hours of fun, they undoubtedly caused problems in my marriage (and their own as well), and they led me along the not so merry road to alcoholism. Of course, I should have known better – joining their bad behaviour was my own choice and a very bad choice it was. I was supposed to be a leading professional accountant with a reputation to match. Instead, I was becoming a heavy-drinking embarrassment.

Monty moved to Antibes in the South of France where his presence in the yacht marina was soon felt. We visited him in his charming apartment near Grasse, on several occasions. He continued drinking and smoking heavily until his eventual demise around 1995, when his liver gave out. It was the way he wanted it to happen.

Tony Robinson and I saw a lot of each other for some years after we left Malta. He was most certainly a bad influence though I valued him as a drinking companion (never a good idea). His house was near Sandwich in Kent where he lived the life of a reprobate, driving his big Merc from pub to pub. It was tobacco that finally did for him. When his lungs started to pack up, he would keep an oxygen cylinder in his favourite pubs and sit at the bar for hours, drink in hand, oxygen mask on face. He died in his sleep in 1989, a fortuitous end for a pirate.

There were others who seemed to think that Malta was a soft touch for exploitation though usually they ended up badly. The Maltese are a wily and skilful crowd. One of the oldest of the Mediterranean civilisations, situated at the crossroads of that wonderfully varied inland sea, they are an amazing mixture of cultures – Greek, Roman, Phoenician, Turk, Arab, Moor and Egyptian, and the earlier Minoan, Mycenaean and Etruscan. They have existed for many millennia. The earliest prehistoric sites on the island at Hagar Qim go back at least 7,000 years. No wonder they knew how to deal with dodgy foreigners.

They also had close ties with Libya, then under the control of the bizarre but dangerous Colonel Gaddafi. A very different place, I imagined, from the Libya that I had visited fresh from School, some ten years earlier. I considered going over to Tripoli to have a look but thought better of it.

Malta, like so many former British colonies and protectorates that had won independence, retained a degree of British habits, customs and institutions and indeed made them a part of their own upper-class lifestyle. Thus, the British clubs, cricket and polo, British cuisine and British goods such as cars, continued to flourish. It always surprised me that people in Malta, with access to every kind of wonderful Mediterranean food, drink, and culture on their doorsteps, should choose to eat the likes of Heinz tinned spaghetti and drink English bottled beer. Still, that was in 1970. Things are different now - joining the European Union transformed the place.

Eventually of course, the Maltese had enough of being pushed around by foreigners and under their new prime minister, Dom Mintoff, threw most of them out. Our little family and the life we had grown to enjoy, were early casualties. We arrived back in England in 1972, weary, perhaps wiser and in need of a lot of remedial work. Prue and Gordon remained happily in Malta for several more years.

Prue, Malta, 1970

Chapter 27

Gents Who Lunch – Hill Samuel

Perhaps it's the lunch that we had or the lunch that we should have had. But I am, in any case, a most inappropriate man (Stevens)

On our little family's return from Malta, I was, at least in theory, at my most employable stage. I had been a partner in an overseas office of a major international firm – Coopers and Lybrand (now re-branded as PWC). I did in fact quite soon manage to land a good and well-paid job at bankers, Hill Samuel, as Internal Audit manager. It seemed like a great step forward but as so often during this time, my performance did not measure up to their expectations.

The trouble was that they were looking for a person dedicated to assessing and improving their operating systems in a period of massive technical change, whereas I was looking for a position where I could enjoy myself and have long lunches with my cronies. It was never going to work out well, but for a time we tried.

I did actually know quite a lot of people in the City by then and felt that somehow, I was furthering my career by spending a lot of time in pubs and wine bars with them. Self-delusion was running riot.

Big drinkers tend to stick together – it helps the self-delusion when you can see other people behaving the same way as you. At that time (the mid-seventies) there seemed to be quite a lot of other people who were happy to behave the same way as me. I wonder what became of them all – none ring me anymore.

The Banker image, 1974

I hired a team of young auditors at Hill Samuel – they were a keen and eager group and I fear, I led them astray. Or maybe it was the other way round.
In my more sober moments, I started writing and published several articles in accountancy magazines. In spite of my problems, I was ambitious and attended courses and seminars in my free time. One of my colleagues was brilliant at persuading leading figures of the day to come at lunchtimes to address the group of accountants I had joined. I recall meeting Enoch Powell at one of these

occasions. The only advice he gave me: 'always drink a pint of water before you make a long speech – it gives your words a sense of urgency'. It does too, though in my case, it was usually a pint of beer that went down.

It seems to me quite surprising how easy a life as a city gent was in those days – compared to now. Our working hours of 9.30 to 5.00 were strictly followed and long lunch hours were normal for many. My lunching may have taken this to extremes, but I was by no means the only person to do so.

Not only were there wine bars at every street corner (my one-time employers, Coopers the Accountants, even had a wine bar in the basement of their building in the whimsically-named Gutter Lane), but there were also a number of 'clubs' – basically drinking clubs, where you could get around the licensing laws (pubs closed usually at 3.00pm in the city then) and drink all afternoon, if you wanted. And I sometimes wanted.

It does seem appalling now, but our team would sometimes come back to the office from a wine bar session and hold pitched battles in the office, throwing sugar lumps and balls of paper at each other. Deplorable, childish behaviour that was remarkable only because it was allowed to happen for so long.

After such long lunch hours, sometimes getting home on the evening commute was a challenge. Often, if I had to wait for a train at Waterloo, I would drift into one of the bars and perhaps not re-emerge for several hours. Occasionally I would fall asleep on the train, travel past my stop to the terminus and then have to travel all the way back again. I see it all now as an appallingly irresponsible and selfish way of life, one that did great harm to Margie and the children, but at the time, I was just too stupid to see this.

Others, however, were certainly starting to notice. Several friends and colleagues commented on my behaviour, usually in the nicest possible way, and usually I took offence but sadly, no action.

One of my favourite city haunts was the Little Ship Club on the river at Wapping. They served very good, strong real ale and fairly cheap lunches. In this friendly atmosphere I could rebuild my confidence from the previous night's hangover and emerge around three pm reeking of beer and ready to return to Hill Samuel and do battle with all comers.

Chapter 28

The Band Played On - As The Ship Began To Sink

Of the terrible doubt of appearances,
Of the uncertainty after all, that we may be deluded (Whitman)

Despite the shadow that my drinking behaviour was casting over our lives, Margie and I had a lot of very good times while the children were young and growing up. For a start, we had some lovely friends, relations and places to visit. Margie's big sister Deidre and her husband Neil Rosebery at Dalmeny were always welcoming, as were my own big sister Jancis and husband David, in Sutherland.

But besides these, we saw a lot of other relations, such as Francie and Mike in Shrewsbury where daughters Charlotte and Sophie were like big sisters to Alex, Johnnie and later, Annabel too. Shropshire is a great place for picnics and small country pubs. Margie and I once spent an idyllic week cycling around Shropshire staying in small hotels and reciting Housman's poetry to each other, when we were first married.

Other special times were spent in Devon at Beaconside, a hotel run by my cousin Andrew Brand and his wife Thea, who was an old school friend of Margie. Beaconside is a beautiful country house near Bideford and the hospitality and the cooking and the comfort were outstanding. No surprise that we went there as often as we could. The children happily played in the grounds and the pool with the Brand's son Charlie, and the sea was not far away. I confess that for me the bar was a big attraction, and I fear that I depleted their hard earned profits by my excessive alcohol consumption.

The Brands were so kind and so popular that every weekend they seemed to be entertaining their friends rather than taking paying customers.

As I was later to find myself, running a small hotel is a lot harder than it seems and the long hours make it an extremely tiring life. I think Andrew and Thea were glad to sell up after a few years and take some hospitality off their friends for a change. I do remember some of those visits very fondly and regret I did not show my gratitude more at the time

We also spent weekends with Margie's sister Sally and her family in Leamington Spa as well as trips to Colchester and to Yorkshire. To begin with, money was not a problem for us, but slowly that began to change, as my poor work performance and prospects began to affect my income adversely.

During these years of the late seventies and the eighties, I tried my hand as an accountant in practice, a newsagent proprietor and as accountant to a firm of Lloyd's insurance brokers. I could have made a success of all of them were it not for my drinking. Instead, I squandered, lonely as a cloud, the resources I had left. The downhill slide to joblessness, isolation and impecunity gathered speed.

Money is the root of evil, they say, but that doesn't mean it's not a necessity. When we ran out of money, due to my mad behaviour, some good people came to our aid. My very fine friend Peter Lindsay helped us on more than one occasion, which I find quite breathtaking. At another time, a friend in Scotland offered me help when one of the children needed urgent hospital treatment. Mike Eagar was another, despite his limited resources. I have never forgotten such acts of generosity and indeed I should not. Kindness tends to be an underrated grace in these modern times.

By the mid-eighties, I was a functioning alcoholic. I was still working but I needed to drink just to appear normal, and the negative consequences for my marriage, my work, my finances, and my health were obvious. Still, I struggled on, trying to appear happy and successful, desperately justifying the unjustifiable and accepting the unacceptable. Trouble was, I really liked alcohol in spite of the damage it did. I was locked in a Stockholm syndrome with my tormentor, the words of Charles Bukowski ringing in my ears: 'find what you love and let it kill

Chapter 29

Writs At The Ritz – The Arundel Trust

It's all downhill from the hotel -
You walk downhill all day (Seidel)

We had somehow acquired very posh offices in Albemarle Street, off Piccadilly in the West End of London. It felt more like the Wild West at times. Albemarle Street runs into Piccadilly, opposite the Ritz Hotel, which became a useful place for meeting and entertaining wealthy clients, especially those from the Middle East.

Arundel Trust sounds like a venerable and benevolent charity or at least an old-school professional investment vehicle beyond reproach. But it was neither. The company had been formed by some city chancer back in the day and had become redundant. I bought the name and the company for a hundred pounds and paid more for an impressive brass plate to put on the door.

My two fellow directors were lawyers – Nigel Spinks had contacts in the Middle East and Antony Lawson Smith, an Old Etonian, had contacts everywhere. It was a time when London was gaining momentum as a financial centre. Britain had joined the European Union in 1973 and the benefits were showing. London had many advantages for overseas investors, and it was our purpose and our business to steer them through the legal, fiscal and financial maze.

Some of our clients were quite difficult to handle. Often, they were from different cultures and were suspicious of the British way of doing business. Or maybe it was our way of doing business, which sometimes seemed odd even to me. Some Iranian clients were extremely litigious, and the writs would sometimes arrive on an hourly basis. Perhaps London was a good place for this sort of thing, perhaps they were litigious everywhere. I really wasn't too bothered because as usual, I was out to lunch most of the time. But the writs would sometimes reach us, even at the lunch table. Even at the Ritz.

I had upped my game since my city days. Lunch was now something to be planned or rather the day was to be planned around lunch – Brown's, Langan's, The Ritz, Le Caprice, Wheelers - the choice was endless

Felix Sawyer was a Bahamian chancer. He was also attached to the Bahamian Embassy- the two roles were not incompatible because as he cheerfully said, most Bahamians were chancers. With his dark skin, his big smile and his great energy, he was a very likeable guy. He loved gambling, shady deals, designer drugs and of course, beautiful girls. The Playboy club was his idea of heaven and it was just round the corner from our office.

Most playboy club members went there, like Felix, for the gambling, the deals, the drugs and the girls. I seemed to be the only one who went there for lunch. But it didn't matter because Felix liked lunch too, only with drugs and girls in attendance. Which was ok with me. I liked drugs and girls too. I just liked lunch more.

One day, Felix brought a friend named Leo to the Playboy. He was unusual because he didn't seem to like gambling or drugs or girls much. He was also extremely old. I never knew how he came to be friends with Felix. He was, however, extremely rich. He told us so. Over lunch, which Leo didn't eat, we hatched a scheme to get Leo a new Rolls Royce, tax free. Felix would be able to arrange this through the Bahamian Embassy and he had a friend who would make the paperwork right. Leo would have to pay cash up front but the saving in car tax would be enormous. My simple task was to pick up the car's registration document from the DVLA.

All was agreed and Leo paid over the cash. Felix phoned me to say the car was ready and I was to collect the documents from the DVLA which I set off to do. But when I got there, I was interviewed by police who had somehow smelt a rat. Luckily, I was not seen as a person of interest in this squalid affair. I never got the documents, Leo never got his car, we never saw Felix again. Leo never saw his money again either.

Felix was not the only client whose origins were mysterious. Mahmood told us that he came from Saudi Arabia though he was actually, Egyptian. He was the best-tailored man I have ever seen. His suits were exquisite, and he could have graced any shop window around the world by simply standing there like a tailor's dummy. Except he had higher ambitions. He was married to a Princess – a member of the Saudi royal family. This is not perhaps quite as impressive as you might imagine since the House of Saud is estimated to have around 15,000 members. It does, however indicate significant wealth. Mahmood was unusual though in wanting to work to achieve wealth himself rather than simply marry it. He owned a construction company in the Middle East and that of course meant litigation – over planning, employment, machinery malfunction and contractual performance

At about this time, my drinking problem was becoming difficult to hide because I was starting to crave alcohol as, in the words of the psalmist: 'the deer pants for streams of water'. Being a strict Muslim, Mahmoud took a dim view of alcohol, so I used to avoid lunch with him at all costs. He may still be out there litigating, still beautifully dressed and calm. One day I vanished, to go into rehab. I don't know how they explained to him what had happened.

Chapter 30

The White Room – Rehab To Redemption (Sunday Post Article)

He seems (uncursed with reason) not to know
The depth or the duration of his woe (Smith)

My battle with addiction is a recurring cliché that leads the reader to boredom, and I apologise for that, but it is part of what I am and therefore cannot be hidden. The Sunday Post, a popular Scottish newspaper, some years ago put it quite well, I believe.

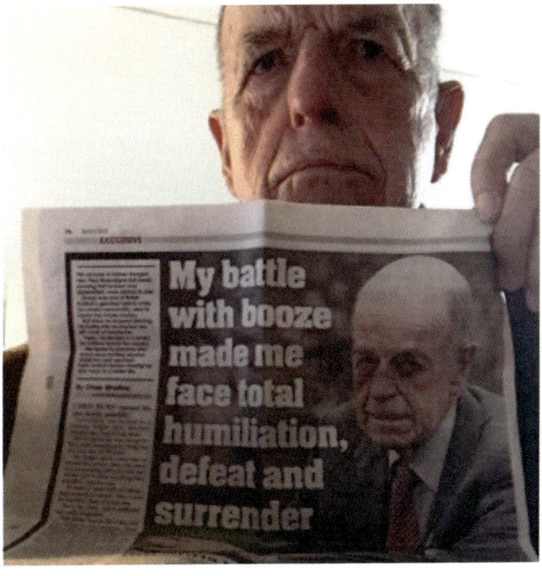

Sunday Post article, 2014

I cant remember why they chose to interview me, it must have been a slow news day.

Chris Burn opened his eyes slowly, painfully.

He was in a white room, bathed in a radiant, bright light. Where was he? How had he ended up there? His first thought was that he was dead. But in reality he was taking the first steps towards truly living for the first time in more than 30 years.

The white room was in an alcohol rehab clinic, the last one his wife would drive him to after bundling him, paralytic, into her car. He was 47 years old and drinking himself to death. This could be his final chance to survive his battle with addiction.

Speaking to Chris it's clear from his refined accent and gentle, well-spoken nature that he hails from good stock. "I came from a very nice family," he concedes. "We were all well behaved, my three older sisters and I "nobody drank too much." I was well brought up and went to a good public school - Ampleforth College in Yorkshire."

Brought up by an aunt, he squarely pins the blame for his long battle with addiction on shyness and social anxiety.

"From the age of 14 onwards I was socially inadequate, and I discovered one day at 15 that drink would help with that. I couldn't pull the girls and a drink or two sure made it easier." It's a story that will be familiar to many. The young lad needing a hit of Dutch courage to help lubricate the wheels of teenage love. But what began as a few drinks to steel the nerves quickly slipped into more dangerous territory.

By the time Chris left his teens he was having at least one drink every day. In his early 20s he was drinking heavily at lunchtimes and in the evening every day. A perforated ulcer at the age of 24 should perhaps have been a warning signal, but at the time no one made the connection. And Chris was enjoying himself far too much to stop. He'd trained to be a chartered accountant and by the time he was 26 he had a very good, high-flying job, living in Paris and working for an international accountancy firm.

His new wife became anxious fairly soon, and as Chris's behaviour became ever more bizarre and drink-fuelled she became progressively more unhappy. They had three children over the next few years, and Chris says: "She was doing the right thing all the time, while I was doing more and more of the wrong thing."

There was absenteeism, drinking late after work and risky situations, including being chased by police around London after being spotted driving erratically, waking in the middle of the night on a bench in Waterloo Station and coming-to on commuter trains miles from where he was meant to be.

At work things were becoming strained, too. "I was a manager at that time and promoted the idea of 'work hard, play hard'. Playing hard included long lunch hours in the wine bar. "But if you're a Chartered Accountant and p***ed half the time you can't add up. It was a recipe for disaster. The number of mistakes I made was horrendous." After being confronted by colleagues, Chris agreed to go into residential treatment in 1983, aged 43.

But nothing changed. "I wouldn't face up to reality," says Chris, looking back. "Alcoholism is such a strange thing "you're in huge trouble but tell yourself you can handle things." Aware he had a problem, but being convinced by those demons that he could take it, that it would all be okay? After leaving rehab, life went rapidly downhill for Chris. He attended five different clinics and was hospitalised twice with liver failure, but still he merrily told himself he could stop when he wanted to. Eventually he hit rock bottom.

"I was without a job and a family, living in one room with lot of empty whisky bottles, drinking two bottles or more a day. "My wife had almost washed her hands of me, but she was the one who came to check up on me and drove me to one last rehab." There, he woke up in the white room, not quite dead yet.

He embarked on a "12 step programme", of the kind used by organisations like Alcoholics Anonymous. It was to be the saving of him. Chris explains, "The 12 Steps help you face reality, provides help to make the changes and gives you a degree of spirituality to fill the gap that is left by the absence of booze." A year after leaving rehab, Chris was taken on as financial director of the new Castle Craig Hospital, one of Scotland's leading private residential drug and alcohol rehabilitation clinics, in Peeblesshire.

After taking a break to run his own hotel in Peebles ("It was helpful to stand behind the bar and see how boring and annoying people become after a few drinks, "says Chris) he returned to the clinic in 2004 to train as a therapist, helping others to overcome the same problems he faced.

I ask him about his lowest point, and he returns to the white room. "I faced total humiliation, defeat and surrender. For me, I had to get to that stage before I could face reality." That reality is now positive.

Chapter 31

Faith, Hope And Charity - Alex, Johnnie And Annabel

Your life was ours, which is with you.
Go on your journey. We go too (Fuller)

I have three children. I remember each of their births, though all were Caesarian. I remember some of their childhood and little of their teen years. I was preoccupied with myself too much and with my self-created problems. Painful to say it now, but true. Such neglect should have had negative results for them. Miraculously, it did not, indeed quite the opposite.

Philip Larkin famously said that 'man hands on misery to man' and I certainly tried my best to do this but seem to have failed. My children appear to have rejected my misery.

When I sobered up in 1987, I still saw too little of them to be properly connected, as a father should be. Too often, I simply wasn't there when they needed me. Yet, when I see them now, I feel proud and humble at the same time. Proud that they have done so well and achieved so much success in lives that have not been easy. And humble that they still care for their selfish old dad who presented them with such a horribly challenging childhood.

Annabel, Johnnie, Alex, 2004

Alex is over fifty years old now and is everything that I was not – honest, dependable, and hardworking, a loving husband and father. A kind of reverse mirror image. He must have learned from my mistakes – at a time when I certainly wasn't doing so. In his late teens and early twenties, he sometimes looked sad and lost and my heart went out to him, and I was so happy when he married his dear Jo. It was as if he had finally found security and a role for himself where he could thrive and blossom, as indeed he has. With his three children Alfie, Ben, and Olivia on the cusp of adulthood, he must be rightly proud of a good job almost done, and I feel proud for him. When I think of him, the good old English word Faith comes to my mind.

Johnnie was born in Malta, at the British Naval Hospital. With its warm climate and beaches, Malta was a lovely place to bring up children. Coming back to the UK must have been a shock. So must some of my behaviour. Young Johnnie could be a bit of a rebel and I can understand why. But he was not one to flinch from a challenge. He went to Emanuel School in Clapham where he was well liked and which I think was extremely good for him. He excelled at rowing for the school and smoking on the 337 bus. And networking, from a young age. His character to me, is more mercurial than his brother's – I think he experiences more ups and downs in his mood. But I think he finds inspiration in many places – his friends, his family, his work and also his frustration. Much creativity comes from frustration, and he has plenty of both.

He has special gifts, and he knows how to use them. With young Oscar and Sophie, he and his dear wife Cathy are the embodiment of parental involvement.

His strength and hope has carried him a long way and it will surely take him further.

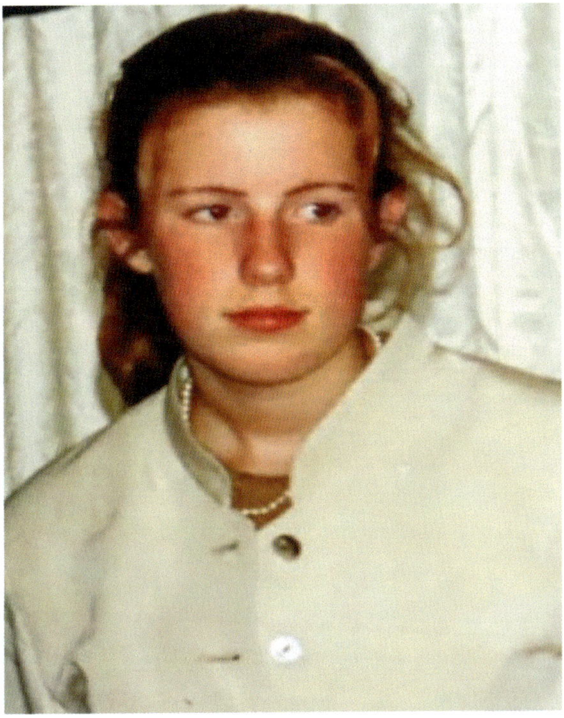
Annabel, 1994

Annabel came into our lives a few years later when my general deterioration had gathered pace, and I think she suffered from it badly. She went for two years as a boarder, to New Hall School, in Essex, at a difficult time in her life, and stayed for two years.

She then returned to continue schooling locally in Richmond. School of any kind was not easy for her and I think she felt very lost and unsupported. At a time when she needed a lot of help, I was not there for her, and her general education suffered from lack of direction, as I think she would herself agree. Nevertheless, her high intelligence, sunny personality and unique sense of humour got her through. She worked at several demanding jobs before making a career-changing decision to start her own business, and what a success she has made of it. Because she has a kind and loving personality, she has suffered in the past from contact with less pleasant people. On the other hand, when dealing with animals, particularly dogs and horses, she can communicate in a way that few others can match. That doesn't mean that she can't handle relationships – she and Rob are a strong couple who work well as a team, and I love to see them both happy together. Furthermore, she has explored and delights in the discovery of her own spirituality and the whole new dimension that this gives to one's life. She is a true seeker into the meaning of it all. There is only one word to describe someone with so much love to give, and that is the good old English word – Charity.

Alex and Johnnie, 1972

People say: "the first half of your life is ruined by your parents and the second half is ruined by your children". My kids have been kind enough to demur about the first bit and I most certainly refute the second.

Good on them, they make me proud.

Chapter 32

A Masterclass – Mike And Francie

And you are not the pine-scented air.
There is just no way that you are the pine-scented air (Collins)

Margie's twin sister, Francie was married two years before us. They made a delightful couple and were always highly supportive of us, even in our darkest hours. More importantly, they were highly supportive of each other. Their relationship was strong because it was built not just on sentimental notions of romance but on a sense of common purpose too.

Mike and Francie 1964

The first time that the four of us met was in a London pub in 1965. Margie and I would shortly be going off to Paris to work and live. But this was just a minor social meeting. Mike, without any preamble gave me a resumé of Francie's good points and the things to watch out for, presumably assuming that both twins' characters were identical, which wasn't actually the case. He finished this brief revue by saying "of course, they're both on the pill", something I had not been aware of!

Francie then said: "everyone knows that Margie has a very soft heart, more stewed mushrooms than gold, but the effect is roughly the same." How right she was.

Mike was about seven years older than us and I often thought of him as a big brother which was fine, because I had always wanted a brother. He sometimes assumed a superior air, but I realised that this was in fact learned behaviour – perhaps a useful weapon on sporting occasions such as cricket, when a batsman faces down a bowler.

Francie of course was easy for me to get on with and she became like a second mother to Alex and Johnnie when they were very young. A genuinely sweet person, she could also stand up for her principles and was a tigress when looking after the interests of her two children, Charlotte and Sophie.

She was an expert in motivating people to get things done, in the nicest possible way. I remember visiting them in Shrewsbury one weekend and spending two days enthusiastically redesigning their garden, orchestrated by Francie. I returned to London on Sunday evening deeply fulfilled but exhausted.

Mike was very good with children and his career in teaching highlights his huge achievements. He was also a great sportsman who had played cricket for Gloucestershire and Ireland. In his first match for Ireland, playing the West Indies, he caught out Gary Sobers. Mike was delighted but his captain said: "You fool! They came here to watch Sobers bat, not you to catch him out!" He also played hockey for Oxford. He would take me golfing at every opportunity and would beat me, but it would always be an entertaining outing.

He was also vastly knowledgeable about National Hunt racing, his other passion. He could talk for hours on handicapping and the vagaries of different courses. He also loved betting, though always in moderation. I'm not sure if he showed a profit but given the time he devoted to the study of form, I would hope so.

Mike's daughter Sophie wrote in a piece for his old school magazine, The

Rugbeian: "He had great drive and determination – as well as high principles and a very kind heart. He brought these qualities, along with a genuine passion for helping teenagers find their paths in life, to his years as a housemaster at Shrewsbury School."

Indeed, I recall many happy visits to Ingrams, the Shrewsbury School house where Mike and Francie lived with daughters Charlotte and Sophie. Our boys Alex and Johnnie loved going there.

Francie, who was devoted to Mike but not particularly interested in sport, produced a series of wonderful children's books that are beautifully written and timeless. My favourite is "The Dolphin of the Two Seas" that she wrote after a visit to us in Malta, where we were then living.

Francie died in 1978, aged just thirty-eight. She had contracted Hodgkin's Lymphoma several years earlier and though she received excellent treatment, the struggle took a toll that she eventually could not overcome. She died at home in Ingrams. It was a very, very sad time for Mike and the girls, and also for poor Margie who lost a twin and a soulmate.

Mike and the children later moved to Cheshire where in 1981, he married again, to Susie Wigley. They had one daughter, Jessica.

Mike may sometimes have seemed to people to be aloof and judgemental, but to us he was the opposite. Whenever we were in trouble of any kind, he would somehow get to know. Then the phone would ring, and it would be Mike, offering advice or more practical solutions. He helped us with money once, he gave us the use of a car. Again, on another occasion, he helped me with a job opportunity. There are people who will sometimes help if shamed or bullied into doing so. With Mike it was always spontaneous, and he has my deepest respect and affection. He died in 2019 surrounded by his family. A very fine man indeed.

Chapter 33

The Year The Sky Fell In - 1978

Out of the night that covers me
Black as the pit from pole to pole (Henley)

In a lifetime you live through some good years and some bad ones. But hopefully, none as awful as the year 1978 was for our family.

It would likely have been a miserable year anyway, since I was drinking heavily, and my work performance was execrable. I was trying to succeed as a Chartered Accountant with my new partners at Wenham, Major and Clarke, but that's a hard thing to do when you're full of booze. They were beginning to treat me in a way that I recognised – with caution, fear, and disdain.

It was a year of death, when significant figures in Margie and my lives all seemed to die within a very short time. First to go was Auntie Prue, the kindest and most uncomplaining of people who must have worried about us terribly but never criticised. She was hospitalised with severe stomach problems and died quite quickly after an operation that was unsuccessful. I was stricken with remorse and unhappy for a long time. I was also quite drunk at her funeral, in the little parish church in Spofforth, where she lived and now lies buried. Gordon, her husband, carried on living in Spofforth for another five or six years after her death, but Yorkshire was never to seem the same.

Margie became quite ill with pneumonia in the spring of that year and her Aunt Betty very kindly stepped in to help look after the children while Margie lay bedridden upstairs, probably stressed out by my behaviour. I received a phone call one morning from her sister Deidre in Scotland, to tell us of the untimely death of Peter Franks, the husband of their other sister Sally in Leamington. Peter was a well known vet in the area and had been unwell for some time. Margie and I and the children had visited them several times.

This was dire news indeed. Poor Sally and their four lovely young children, Liz, Philip, Stephen, and Will were obviously devastated. I went to the funeral which was a difficult affair (Margie was too ill to go). It was a mark of the degree of concern there was in the family about my problems, that Sally, Peter's widow, took time at the reception in the midst of her own terrible grief, to give me a talking to about the need to mend my ways. The poor girl was quite right to do so of course, though I didn't appreciate it at the time, such was my denial.

The Reids with their mother, Dalmeny 1977

Worse was to come however – dear Francie had been ailing for a long time and by early summer she was desperately weak though still trying to put up a brave show. She had been going to see a very well-known and respected faith healer called Bruce McManaway and together they had made some progress, but now she seemed to be feeling that her time was coming. Mike rang one evening to warn us and Margie and the children went up to Shrewsbury the next day by train. Poor Francie died that evening and Margie was with her. I went up the following day and the school-house, where we had had such happy times, was a very sad place. It was still term-time, but the atmosphere was quiet and subdued.

The big weeping willow tree in the garden, which the boys used to hide under to smoke, mysteriously started to wither and die that same day.

A week or so later, Francie was buried in the nuns' graveyard at New Hall School in Essex, the place where she and Margie had had happy and supportive times when their young lives were under the strain of their parents' divorce. It was a lovely sunny June day and all the flowers were blooming. A setting more suitable for a wedding than a funeral, but that's how it goes sometimes.

The grim reaper was not finished with us yet. Towards the end of the summer, Margie's mother, Mary who had had a stroke some years before, also died. This was perhaps a release for the poor woman, but I felt so sad for Margie that she had to bear so many blows in such a short time. Mary had been living in Kilmacolm, near Glasgow, with her second husband Ronald, a charming and kindly retired lawyer. She had finally found happiness again for a few years, after the stressful divorce from Ronnie.

Poor Mary had spent a lot of unhappy years after her divorce from Ronnie in 1961. For a long time, she seemed unable to settle down in any particular place, living at various times in Wales, Scotland and Dorset. She had clearly been devastated by the upheaval caused by the divorce, both emotionally and in practical terms. She remained however, a very nice and entertaining person, but someone in desperate need of a meaningful relationship. It was thus a real delight when she met and married her second husband Ronald Morris. The few years they had together must have given her great happiness.

By the end of 1978 we were sad, bloody but unbowed. Our lives felt diminished, as indeed they had been, but the only option was to soldier on, which is what we did.

Chapter 34

The Bethlem Philistines – Rehab Denial Days

In me the tiger sniffs the rose.
Look in my heart, kind friends, and tremble (Sassoon)

"So, how do you feel about that?" Those words are the mantra of every therapist I have ever met, and I suppose they always will be. But they stink. Why? Because a therapist really doesn't give a toss how you are feeling. They already know you are in huge emotional turmoil, otherwise you wouldn't be in therapy (unless you are one of the rare psychos that occasionally slips through the net). No, the therapist doesn't care, they are just trying to squeeze a reaction out of you, because their aim is simple. Your goal is self-discovery. And the way to self-discovery is to learn from your own reactions. Hence the eternal question – "how do you feel about that".

In rehab, therapy is a sledgehammer used to crack a nut (!). Provided the nut – the patient - is compliant, they will be opened-up, ground down and squashed sideways then gurgitated back into society. It works surprisingly well. Very few David's can beat such a Goliath.

It's actually a very simple recipe for success that was formulated by the Ancient Greeks, who knew plenty about drunkenness and drug use (Homer's lotus-eaters were our dope-heads). The Greeks invented the word 'therapy' after all.

The temple of Apollo at Delphi (aka the Delphic Oracle) was the world's first rehab. On its walls were slogans: 'Water is Best', 'Nothing in Excess' and 'Know Thyself'. Words such as these can only have been written by an addiction therapist.

The temple was also a centre for the cult of Dionysus, god of wine and drunkenness. The ancients didn't just go there to get their fortune told – they went to be dried out and rehabilitated. But, just like today, the Delphi experience didn't always work. Take that notorious drunkard, Alexander the Great – he attended at Delphi, demanding the usual treatment, before his world-beating expedition. The reluctant priestess (ie. therapist), eventually declared that he would be 'invincible'. This was what Alexander wanted to hear, and he left happy and confident. In spite of his drinking, Alexander had great military success but died from alcoholic poisoning aged only 32. He had indeed been invincible – unable to conquer himself and his addiction.

While languishing in rehab myself, at London's august Bethlem Hospital for the mentally ill, I amused myself thus, with these arcane theories about the ancient Greeks. It was better than facing up to my real problems, and more fun. I felt like David ranged against the Philistines of the NHS system and in my arrogance, I reckoned that I could beat them. Somehow, in spite of my terrible character defects, I felt invincible, just like Alexander.,

As for my theories about the Delphic Oracle Rehab, I explained them at length to the Venezuelan psychiatrist in charge of my treatment. It freaked him out so much that he sectioned me for a further month. Philistines are everywhere.

Chapter 35

Clouds And Castles - Peter And Margaret Ann McCann

Resign my life for this life, my speech for that unspoken,
The awakened, lips parted, the hope, the new ships (Eliot)

At the start, there seemed to be awful misconceptions at our every meeting. The first time we met, my strange, deluded ego made me think myself a charismatic entrepreneur - come to help them improve their rehab business - such was my grandiosity and denial. They, on the other hand, could plainly see me as a hopeless alcoholic desperately needing treatment, not to be trusted to run a tap in a toilet. I couldn't leave fast enough. The meeting was short.

The second time we met, I became convinced that she was the Virgin Mary and he, in his striped shirt and spotted bow tie, was a bizarre but dapper manifestation of Satan. I was having the DTs at the time so I couldn't run away, but it didn't stop me trying. I got as far as the floor.

At our third meeting I was in severe alcoholic withdrawals and shaking like Al Jolson singing Mammy, only I wasn't singing, I was crying. Margaret Ann put an arm round me and told me it was ok. It certainly didn't feel ok, but it turned out that she was right, and thirty-five years later, it is still ok.

Peter and Margaret Ann McCann founded Clouds House in Wiltshire, the rehab that got me sober. They went on to found Castle Craig Hospital in Scotland, the rehab where I worked from the day it began, for on and off thirty years. They have been in the recovery business for nearly fifty years and have treated close to twenty thousand patients, many with successful outcomes. They know what they are doing, and they do it supremely well. I owe them more than gratitude - I owe them my life.

Peter and I were at boarding school together where we knew each other without I would say, being close friends. We were in different houses, on different academic paths. It was quite a shock to meet him again at Clouds. Especially with the Satan angle, though I didn't mention that until I was sure it wasn't true.

The McCann's were what I needed. They knew that you simply cannot compromise with addiction and they followed this rule at all times, without any deviation. It was perfect therapy for the likes of me who had spent a lifetime trying to get away with murder. Tough love was their approach and it worked. No 'good cop – bad cop' with them, it was 'bad -cop' all the way but delivered with empathy and compassion.

Being at Clouds was like boarding school all over again only different. They didn't beat you if they didn't like your behaviour, they had more subtle ways of getting you to change, and at Clouds House, the big word was 'change'. It was horribly painful at times because, when you've been a twat for thirty years and denying it, the act of facing up to it is bound to be agonising. But, as the Delphic Oracle well understood, knowing oneself is the key to recovery. There was no gain without pain at Clouds House, but by the time I left, I was a different person, and it felt good. I felt I was changing.

But better was to come. Although I was quite anxious and fragile in my early years of recovery from addiction, Peter and Margaret Ann were prepared to trust me. A year after leaving Clouds, Peter rang me and asked if I would help them start their new rehab project in Scotland. I was more than happy to oblige and together we found a suitable site - Castle Craig, the perfect place, in beautiful countryside, the ideal location in many ways. We raised the finance needed, hired the staff and opened for business on 1st October 1988. Looking back on it all I am still amazed. Not that we did it, but that they trusted me enough to join them. It was a huge show of confidence that meant an awful lot to me at that difficult time in my life. And today it still means a lot.

Going to work at Castle Craig was perfect for my recovery because it meant that I was continually supported by right minded people. And there were no temptations. On the other hand, it took me to Scotland, a long distance away from Margie and the children. Yet the truth was that, due to my behaviour, I was legally banned from living with them, in their new house in Richmond. A document of separation had been drawn up and signed, and I had nowhere to go. Except, as it now turned out, Scotland.

Although English, I have lived in Scotland for thirty years. Recently I have returned to London. I like both places but for different reasons. I also quite like living in both places at once, though the travelling can be irksome. Over the years, I have made the trip North across the border and back hundreds of times

Most of my friends are now in Scotland and my work has been there too for the past thirty-five years.

My dentist, bridge club, poetry group and AA group are in Scotland. My family and my doctor are in London. I have a roof above my head in both countries. It sounds very leisured and even self-indulgent, but it is all done on a shoestring. I own no property and have no valuables in either location. Yet I am happy that.

I know kind, amusing and wise people in England and Scotland - I count myself fortunate. London is where my family live and as I get older, nothing else seems to matter. But Scotland has a special place in my heart because it's where my recovery really began.

What do I think of Scottish independence? I think they should give it a try, if that is what the majority want. A Scotland that is independent and also part of the EU could be a success and even if not rich could survive economically as an EU member. It's a better idea than the Darien scheme of 1778.

Chapter 36

My Guardian Angel – St Bernadette

My faithful friend that shall be mine,
Unfailing, till my death (Newman)

If somebody had told me fifty years ago that I would be writing about a guardian angel, I would have scoffed loud and long. This tells me how much I have changed. I do not think I would be alive today if it were not for St Bernadette. She is my guardian angel, and I am so glad.

It started nearly twenty years ago. I had just sold my hotel in Scotland and had a little free time – something that I had not had for ages. I arranged to go on a pilgrimage to Lourdes – not just a quick inspection visit like a tourist. No, I arranged to go with the puissant and doughty-sounding Knights of Malta, on a full-blown week-long pilgrimage. This was the real thing, the full menu experience. I had no idea what to expect, but I soon found out.

Our virtuous quest began at Stansted airport, where we waited for hours. As it was a proper pilgrimage there were lots of sick (ie disabled) people to load on the plane. Eventually we were all aboard.

The Knights of Malta are a very Catholic, very rich and frankly quite snooty bunch of people. You only get to be a Knight if they like you and also if you pay a considerable sum of money. No chance for me then, not that I was bothered. They certainly weren't bad people, just rather exclusive and lofty. Not being either rich or upper class (a lot of them are very aristocratic by birth), I felt excluded by many, though not all of them. Nevertheless, I persevered. I am, after all a naturally reclusive person, burdened with latent Uriah Heep syndrome.

On the plane to Lourdes from Stansted, I sat next to a very nice lady who seemed to be a missionary in South Africa. She told me about her life and work in a very remote part of that large country and it sounded fascinating and the flight went quickly. Eventually we arrived at our destination where there was more work helping the malades (the sick) to get settled. This was followed by prayers in the basilica and bed.

The next four days were repetitive and quite hard work, helping the malades at the hospital and around the whole site, together with mass, processions and prayer meetings. I spent more time praying than I ever have. I can't say I enjoyed it, I felt tired and lonely and insecure. I was way out of my comfort zone.

Sometimes I went exploring on my own and learned a lot about St Bernadette and her little companions, and the series of visions that she saw. It was a very sweet and moving story. St Bernadette was not believed at first, when she spoke about her visions, and I realised that she too must have felt very tired, lonely and isolated. Since nobody was talking to me much, I tried doing some more praying and meditating. I also tried talking to St Bernadette herself. Nothing really happened, though I found it calmed me down.

One of the knights told me that St Bernadette always 'gives you a present' when you do the pilgrimage. I was sceptical and wondered if I would get anything. It came time to leave, we flew back to Stansted and I said goodbye to the nice lady from South Africa and no one else much, then ran for the car park. Soon I was home.

I continued my daily conversations with St Bernadette and found that they were giving me a sense of peace and calm that I had never experienced before. I found that if I told her my troubles she listened and I found that if I needed strength, she was there to help me through difficult situations.

Here are some examples: I was unemployed yet I found work, I had big financial problems but they got sorted out, I had nowhere to live (having ceased being a hotelier) and a friend came to my help. In addition, my relationship with Margie started getting better, I saw more of my children, and I began consciously trying to become a better person. In moments of doubt and indecision, all I needed was to ask myself: what would St Bernadette do in this situation? And I always had an answer. Because she would always do the right thing. As the knight had predicted to me at Lourdes, she had given me a present.

I have returned to Lourdes three times since then, once alone, once with my daughter Annabel who loved it, and once with Margie who I think, liked it and enjoyed the experience, though her cognitive powers were not what they had once been.

St Bernadette was 14 when she saw her first vision. She struggled with ill health throughout her short life. At age 21 she joined the convent of the Sisters of Charity at Nevers where she died in 1879 aged just 35. Her death was due to tuberculosis of the lungs and bones, particularly her left knee. She lies in the chapel of the convent in Nevers. So, I thought I had better do a pilgrimage there as well. And I did.

I've actually been to Nevers three times and the trip has not always gone well. The first time, I worked out after much study of timetables, that I could actually travel there from Scotland, and back, in one day. Rather rashly, I decided to try. It involved flying to Paris, then train to Nevers, an hour at the convent then back to Paris for the evening flight back to Scotland. It nearly worked. But agonisingly, the train was fifty minutes late getting to Nevers. This meant I had just ten minutes to get to the convent, say a prayer and get back on the Paris train. It simply wasn't possible in ten minutes as the convent was a long way from the Rail station. I wasted a day's travel for nothing, at some expense, and vowed to do better next time.

A year later, I had more success because I stayed at Peter Lindsay's Paris flat and easily travelled down to Nevers and back. It was a memorable experience to see Bernadette's tiny body lying in a glass case in the convent church.

I felt great when I left the peaceful convent to walk back to the train station – I had done what I intended, and I was proud of myself. St Bernadette should be pretty pleased with me too, I thought as I crossed the busy main street of the little French town. Bang! I found myself lying flat on my face in the middle of the road. The traffic screeched to a stop and I tried to get up. My knee (which already was a problem) had somehow collapsed and been badly twisted and I could hardly walk. I had to buy a stick for support and somehow got the train back to Paris. I was upset and angry. What had happened? I thought about it a lot on the train. It was, I think, a reminder that life isn't that simple. It's not a case of ticking boxes and getting a result. St Bernadette herself had not had an easy life. She had died in great pain. In fact, the worst pain for her had been in the left knee, as it now was for me. I had been given a useful and firm reminder: keep the big picture in mind – my life plan for self-improvement with divine help, was still very much work in progress.

Back in Scotland some weeks later, I happened to see in the newspaper an account of the murder of a missionary in South Africa by unknown robbers. It was the lady that I had talked to on the plane, on my first trip to Lourdes. Mysterious are the ways of the Lord.

Clearly, there is a power for evil in the world as well as a power for good. St Bernadette is for me a guide through life's dangers and a direct connection to all the good that there is. For some, this may be far-fetched. It works for me and I am grateful for Bernadette whose example of humility, honesty, piety and love has inspired so many people who can see how much can be achieved with just these simple things.

Chapter 37

The Fearless Four - And A Dog Named Bonnie

I knew when I met you
An adventure was going to happen (Milne)

When I started working and living at Castle Craig, Annabel was nine years old and she used to like coming up to stay. I lived then in a cottage in the grounds and there were fifty acres of grass, woods and old buildings to be explored. Peter and Margaret Ann lived in another cottage nearby with their four young children Victoria, Dominic, Felicity and Peter whose ages then ranged from two (Peter) to eight (Victoria). They basically formed a gang of four together because young Peter was really too small to be included, at first anyway. The children really enjoyed roaming round the estate which was safe but exciting at the same time. They called themselves the Fearless Four (later expanded to Five when young Peter joined).

After a year in Scotland, I acquired a young Collie pup from Tom, a local farmer friend. I had never owned a dog before, and it was a brilliant experience. With Bonnie for company, I had reason to go walking all over the local countryside which I came to enjoy greatly. Later we even tackled some Munros (hills of over three thousand feet) together.

Of course, the children loved having Bonnie around and the feeling was no doubt mutual. The fearless four as they called themselves, would be out for hours exploring and just having a good time.

Annabel and Bonnie, 1993

I had never had a dog of my own before Bonnie came along and I have never had another one. The experience was so good and left me quite bereaved, so perhaps I am frightened of repeating the cycle. Bonnie was born in a shed on a farm by the river Clyde in Lanarkshire – a really hard country background. Her brother, most aptly named Clyde, was shot by his farmer owner because he took to chasing sheep. It was that sort of farm.

Bonnie was a true Collie. Very much a one-man dog, she was highly biddable, strong, loyal, protective and enthusiastic. She went with me everywhere and never strayed far though she would happily go off with the children, if I said it was ok. She was devoted to all our family but especially to Annabel and Margie. She brought a lot of new dynamics into our lives and it was good for us. I won't go on.

Her father had lived to the amazing age of twenty-five and was featured in the Scottish Farmer as Scotland's oldest sheepdog. But Bonnie only managed 16 years. She got a wee bit irascible in her old age but then, most of us do. Taking her to the vet for the last time was tough.

The Fearless Four ranged the grounds with Bonnie for several years and became the Fearless Five when young Peter grew old enough to join. The old graveyard, the walled garden, the site of the ancient castle on top of the hill, and the field containing the small black Orkney sheep, were all familiar places where I might find them when out for a walk myself.

Castle Craig Estate, 2019

Here is a poem written by Annabel aged ten - I think it's pretty good

This Morning I Woke Up With Snow

A fresh white blanket of snow

Small footprints from where

The kitten has been playing

The foulness of my boots biting my toes,

Getting knocked out by a snowball -

How bitter!

The wee mole catches a cold

along with the mouse's tail -

Hail and fog, hurting my dog -

What a mean nature we have.

The fearless Four continued to operate for several years. I recently found a record, kept by Annabel. They had a symbol (Tiger) and a flag of their own

(Tiger-coloured), designed by Dominic. The secret password was 'Ooga'. The command structure apparently went like this:

Leader - Annabel

Deputy Head - Victoria

Hero - Dominic

Little Warrior - Felicity

Thinker - Victoria

Bravest - Annabel

Doctor - Felicity

Key Keeper - Dominic.

There was also the dreaded 'Wimp of the Day Chart'. I won't go into more details on that !

Today, the fearless four/five are all successful in their chosen fields of work and leading happy lives. Victoria and Dominic both play important roles in the running of Castle Craig Hospital while Felicity and young Peter are both doctors doing great things in their chosen fields of medicine. Annabel meanwhile, is becoming a specialist in canine and equine behaviours

She still remembers those times with great fondness, quoting the immortal words of Winnie the Pooh: "We didn't realise we were making memories, we just knew we were having fun."

There must be something very therapeutic in the air, in that particular part of Scotland -.not just for children, but for adults and animals as well.

Chapter 38

The Lord And The Lord Lieutenant – The Rosebery's And The Houston's

One equal temper of heroic hearts,
Made weak by time and fate, but strong in will (Tennyson)

I have been visiting Scotland regularly, almost annually since I was a child. So has Margie. So has the Queen for that matter and lots of other people. Our photograph albums of the forties and fifties see us all clad in raincoats posing grumpily, sometimes picnicking in what looks like a heather bog somewhere 'up North', or else perhaps standing beside a big black gun at Edinburgh Castle, the cobblestones glistening in the rain. Even the Queen can't control Scottish weather, so I expect her albums look much the same as mine.

In between grumpy posings, we had a jolly nice time, usually. This was mainly due to there being a lot of relations living North of the Border and in the case of my sister Caroline, almost bang on the Border itself, at Longtown, near Gretna.

Deirdre and Neil, 2019

We spent many Christmases with the young children at Dalmeny House outside Edinburgh, where Margie's elder sister Deirdre and her husband Neil, Lord Rosebery, were unfailingly hospitable.

It was also exciting to be surrounded by the astonishing paintings and the beautiful furniture and other works of art, some of huge national value. Deirdre knows the story behind each piece and has travelled the world

giving talks on the subject, so it was wonderful to be given the personal tour. I'm not sure how many guests enjoy Deirdre and Neil's hospitality each year, but their visitor's book must run to many volumes.
Margie's brother David, with his wife Chrissie and their family returned from Hong Kong when the children were quite small. They were often at Portmore House, outside Peebles – South of Edinburgh, and were another source of generous hospitality and some very memorable parties.

Another of the pleasures of being in Scotland for me was being able to see a lot of my eldest sister Jancis and her husband David Houston. When I arrived in Scotland in 1988, to live and work at Castle Craig, I would often drive up the A9 past the grim battlefield of Culloden Moor, past Inverness and on into Sutherland, to stay with them for the weekend. Again, there was always a lavish welcome here in this distant, sparsely populated country. They had retired to Scotland about the year 2000, after David's distinguished career in the army ended. He retired a Major General with a CBE for his good service, especially notable in Northern Ireland where he commanded the Londonderry Brigade at a difficult time in that Island's history.

Jancis and David, 2010

The Houston's two sons, Simon and Angus were the same age as Alex and Johnnie and they got on so well that it was a delight to see them together, and they are all still good friends. In the summer they could go camping and they loved going to the sea as well, both the West and East coasts.

David and I would go fishing either on the magnificent river Oykel which was yards from their front door, or one of the many lochs in the area – we were spoilt for choice really. Also, we would play golf. David was a member at beautiful Royal Dornoch, a magnificent championship course that was far too demanding for our limited skills – we would go very early in the morning, so there would not be anyone to see how badly we were playing.

They lived at Rosehall in Sutherland where David was for many years the Lord Lieutenant. This of course meant that they knew everyone in the county and beyond so we, when we were staying, were constantly going out to the houses of the great and the good in the area

David and Jancis died within months of each other, after sixty years of very happy marriage. They are both buried at nearby Invershin, beside the Oykel, overlooked by the huge bulk of Carbisdale Castle - exactly where they were happiest. David liked to tell the story of a winter burial at that same place. Rain was slanting in as the minister spoke, at great length, of the eventual damnation facing the mourners. Noticing water running off the life-worn nose of the man standing next to him, David had muttered, "This is interminable." The man, a very old highlander, replied, very quietly: "Aye, I was beginning to wonder if it was worth my while going home."

Chapter 39

Hotel Salmagundi – The Kingsmuir Hotel, Peebles

Through open doors, the dining-room declares
A larger loneliness of knives and glass (Larkin)

The word salmagundi is derived from the French word salmigondis, which means a disparate assembly of things, ideas or people, forming an incoherent whole (Wikipedia). The bar of the Kingsmuir Hotel, Peebles, was like that every night. And I couldn't even dull the pain with alcohol. It quickly got head-bangingly boring.

In retrospect, buying the Kingsmuir was a typically questionable life decision, of the kind that had dogged me for too long. With the surprising but fortuitous exception of my marriage, which I have never regretted, I seemed to have got myself into a Sisyphean pattern where 'act in haste and repent at leisure' was my default behaviour. And here it was all over again, and this time I was a recovering alcoholic running a bar, of all places. Déjà vu was beginning to look horribly like nostalgie de la boue.

What had happened was that I had needed to make a statement. After six years in Scotland helping to run an alcohol and drugs rehab, I decided, a touch arrogantly, that I needed a change. I told myself I should get back into a more mainstream style of work, among a more 'normal' type of person. I needed to show the world that I had recovered.

So, needing to make a statement to the world about my rehabilitation as a human being led me to consider self- reincarnation as a hotelier. After all, I thought, running a hotel is very similar to running a rehab, and I'd done that successfully. And the idea of the hotelier is one that in theory, I rather like – the amiable mine host, surrounded with good company and fine fare was just the image I was after. A pillar of the local community too, perhaps. Mr Micawber's rebirth as a person of substance and respect after emigrating to Australia in Dickens' David Copperfield came into my mind. The Kingsmuir would be my Australia, I thought, totally without irony.

Kingsmuir Hotel, Peebles, 1996

Actually, life at the Kingsmuir wasn't all bad by any means. At times, it was extremely enjoyable. I got to know a large number of people in the area and became what the locals called 'a well-kent face' in the town. Many of our customers were extremely nice and interesting individuals. Even today, twenty years later, people stop me in Peebles High Street to say: "oh I wish you hadn't left the Kingsmuir", which produces a nice feeling.

The children used to come up with their friends from London and try to drink the place dry, or so it seemed, which was fine by me and also popular with the regulars who would otherwise get bored with talking to each other day after day. When these young Southerners arrived, usually in the off season, and occupied the hotel, it was a real boost and something I looked forward to a lot.

I was lucky to have two good managers during my ten years of ownership –

firstly Fay Napier who had been a colleague at Castle Craig and who knew all the locals, being a 'gutterbluid' (a born and bred Peebleian - the term came from the many butchers shops in the town). Fay had a network of family members who could help out when staff shortages occurred. She was the most loyal of people and sadly retired due to ill health and died a short time later.

Fay was succeeded by Peggy, who had run hotels in South Africa and brought a new atmosphere and new clientele to the place with her cheerful demeanour. She was popular with staff and customers and she and Rebecca (our chef) and Dot (senior waitress) still meet up at least once a year.

The Kingsmuir had a very loyal following of customers because we provided good service and value for money. Our food won us many awards. We were not a top-class outfit because we never had the money to spend on a big enough upgrade, but we always kept to a high standard and our customers appreciated that.

We were the only licensed premises on the South side of the river which made the bar popular with the locals, especially those who didn't like walking far for their pint. Some locals I got to know pretty well, as you do when you see them every day. Some I liked very much and some I wished I'd never see again. I learnt the downsides of running licensed premises – the drunks, the bores, the people who won't go home, the people who complain about everything, the people who start fights. Every landlord knows what I mean. But they pay their money like everyone else. There are the people I really don't miss.

I began to tire of the Kingsmuir after the first few years. I liked the place and many of the people I saw every day, but the work was hard and repetitive and the lifestyle was very limiting – it was a difficult business to leave for any but a short period of time. Still, I kept going for a while, knowing that I was providing a popular recreational facility in the town as well as employment for a number of people. People seemed surprised that I lasted as long as ten years, but I did enjoy the life.

Finally, I received a good offer for the premises which I eventually decided to take. I felt bad about leaving and what it would mean for the customers and especially for the staff, many of whom had been so loyal. Some of the bar staff had started trying to help themselves to my takings (easily done in a cash business) and that made my mind up. We had a memorable farewell party for our favourite customers and then it was over. The Kingsmuir closed its doors, to reopen shortly afterwards as an upmarket B&B. Our bar regulars, and staff, had to look elsewhere for their needs.

It took me several months to adjust to not running the Kingsmuir Hotel. I had lived the endless routine of serving meals, checking customers in and out and doing all the other familiar activities day after that when it stopped, I was taken by surprise. I was left with a great emptiness.

Chapter 40

The Weary Smile Of Welcome – A Hotelier's Day

Do you remember an inn, Miranda?
Do you remember an inn? (Belloc)

I happened to pick up a hospitality trade magazine the other day and it fell open at a cheery article that started like this: "Which elements of running a hotel do hoteliers enjoy the most? And what motivates them to do a great job as they tackle the day-to-day tasks?" It made me feel grateful that I would never be a hotelier again, never have to bear the repetition, the mindless drudgery and the boredom. For too long, the following became my daily routine -

I rise at 0630 and stagger towards the kitchen. My knee joints ache permanently these days from spending so much time standing. Without having to think. I put the porridge that has been steeping all night, onto a slow heat. I put a pack of twenty bacon rashers in the oven to bake and crisp and get the eggs out of the fridge. When breakfast starts, it can be hectic and I am the only one on duty. This is manageable if we have up to ten guests - any more, and havoc reigns. Hopefully they won't all come at once and I will be able to balance the cooking and serving with checking out the guests that want to leave early. I will have prepared their bills the night before. The timing can be a bit stressful but that's part of the life.

By nine thirty the day staff have arrived, and I am ready for a break and a coffee. The tourist board are coming for an inspection at ten, so I check that the basics have been done- clean toilets, bar floor washed etc. And warn the staff.

Hotelier, 1995

I greet the inspector and walk him round. I have known George Miller several years and his advice has always been invaluable, so I can anticipate what he is likely to look for – clean showers for example, in the bathrooms, so it is all fairly humdrum. We have been through this, many times. George is gone after an hour and the bar is due to open at eleven – there is usually at least one regular gasping for a drink at opening time. I can easily spot the problem drinkers of course – how could I not, with my record. But I have to be very non-judgmental here. It is a hard part of the job that I hadn't expected. The place fills up slowly and at noon we start lunches. I check that the kitchen is doing ok and also that the waiting staff have turned up. The hardest part of the job is dealing with staff and I know I don't do it well. I should leave it to the manager, but I am a compulsive micro-manager.

The next two and a half hours pass quickly as we have a lot of lunches today – it can be hard to anticipate when this sort of rush will happen. I have to turn my hand to a bit of waiting, to help the staff out. I quite like that as you get to talk to the regulars, and some are very nice people.

By two thirty things are quiet again and hopefully I can grab a couple of hours siesta before the evening work starts. But today we have a big, big problem that has suddenly appeared. We are overbooked in the bedrooms. Somebody has taken a booking for a party of four couples and failed to record it in the system, thus the rooms have been let to other customers. The four couples are due to arrive in about an hour's time and we must find them alternative accommodation. We ring round all the hotels in the area and they are full. It is summer, after all, and the Edinburgh Festival is on. The clock is ticking, and the nightmare continues. In the nick of time we find them rooms some distance away and I have to wait for their arrival, so as to break the news to them. It is all very stressful, but it is finally done and now we are near the evening session. The bar starts to fill at five and will continue busy for the next six hours. The barman is efficient, but I have to help out now and then. Besides, I suspect him of skimming the profits and don't like leaving him alone.

My heart sinks as I see some familiar faces in the bar – the heavy drinkers, the troublemakers and worst of all, the really boring ones. They all want a piece of my time, not for anything important, just someone to talk to, but my time is precious and I have to keep slipping away to check that things are going smoothly in the kitchen. By eleven I am dead on my feet, the chatter in the bar has become white noise of which I am barely aware. I am longing for the closing time and for everyone to leave. But they all want to stay. Drinkers always do. It requires all my skills of diplomacy to get them out of the building before midnight. But eventually they are gone. The last of the staff leave, and I am left again alone and in charge.

I lock up, check that the alarms are working, check the car park and finally fall into bed. It is one a.m. and I must be ready to do it all over again tomorrow. I sleep.

It is a hard grind, but one does get used to it. Would it be easier if I was not teetotal, if I drank with the customers? It might be – it would probably be better for business too. But of course, I won't do that. You get used to the life, and I can see why. People like to know you. They view you as a part of their lives. To some, it seems to be an important part. They feel reassured by seeing you day after day. In fact, they become quite possessive. Some people were visibly upset when I stopped being a hotelier, as if a change from the familiar routine in their lives was cause for anxiety and dismay. But for me, it was certainly not.

Chapter 41
Greek Fire – A Cultural Holiday

But we will leave this paltry land, And sail from hence to Greece, to lovely Greece
I'll be thy Jason, thou my golden fleece; Where painted carpets o'er the meads are hurl'd, And Bacchus' vineyards overspread the world, Where woods and forests go in goodly green, I'll be Adonis, thou shalt be Love's Queen (Marlowe)

In the early spring of 2000, Margie and I took a trip to Greece. Amazingly, neither of us had previously spent more than a day there. Apart from the unrivalled culture on display, we really enjoyed the experience. And each other's company too.

Margie wrote this to her sister on her return:
Greece was great! Fags only £1 per packet, booze (not a connoisseur's dream situation actually) so deliciously cheap. Food likewise, if rather 'curate's eggish' in the main dish bits, (we were eating at the bottom end of the market), at least one could rely on yoghurt, honey, feta and Greek salad.

But it was just lovely – we agreed we should have gone long ago. And your Fodor Guide was wonderful: it could not have had more appreciative guardians. All the history and vocabulary stuff it contains, far better than the stuff I had.

We did loads, in a hire car, including going up really heart-stoppingly-hairy mountain bends on barely made roads in the Peloponnese, with snow capped peaks eg Mt Parnassus in view and enjoyed it enormously. Christoff was especially slain by Mycenae, him being a Homer person (we were so lucky, only seven people there, Epidaurus, likewise, was having an off day when we called and was deliciously empty). But at Delphi, and on the Acropolis we met the real tourist world. Mostly, on these 'World Class Sites', we (and the site itself) were pressed upon by streams of Japs, Yanks, Huns, Limeys etc same as one sees outside Mme Tussaud's any summers day in London.

Margie at the Parthenon, 2000

We did a three island trip complete with Greek dancing and so forth, if one wanted it. In the same sort of phalanx of tourists, and did meet some nice people, as we bought our sponges and pistachio nuts.

But yesterday, just at the foot of the overcrowded acropolis, where blokes like Socrates and his chums used to meet, it was all empty; except for birdsong and sweet spring grass and flowers. We picnicked tranquilly and observed, at a mere football field's length, the rest of the foreign hoi polloi in the Plaka, feeding expensively at outside tables and being harassed by Romanians, accordian players and lacework salespersons. Lucky us!

Lucky us indeed, and such an enjoyable week. It was a real spine-tingling experience. To stand at Mycenae and share the view across the plain of Argos to the sea, the view that Agamemnon must once have seen, and equally to be at Thermopylae where the four hundred Spartans so gladly died in 480 BC, that their country might remain free.

Forty-five years earlier as a schoolboy, I had read my Homer and my Thucydides and now they suddenly had a new dimension.

My chief memory is not of ancient sites however, though we saw plenty.

Thanks to the Fodor guide, Margie had read that the Greeks love bargaining and fully expect to be haggled at every opportunity. She was determined to try this out.

In the Plaka (once the red-light district of Athens, but now very chic), she spied a swanky gift shop. Inside, was a bronze ornament priced at 500 euros. Handing the astonished sales lady just fifty euros, she raised her eyebrows and said – ok? heading for the door at the same time. The short period of noisy wrangling that followed did nothing for the cause of Anglo Greek friendship and we left the shop to shouts of φύγε! μην επιστρέψεις (later translated as 'push off - don't come back'.)

We had, it seemed, picked the wrong place. Socrates and his chums might have done better.

Chapter 42

Car Crash - A Scottish Event

As soon as the catastrophe came to be known
The alarm from mouth to mouth was blown (McGonagall)

Everyone knew about this one, it happened on a main road near where I both lived and worked. I knew the farmer whose fence I hit and the people who kindly stopped to give me a lift home. It was quite a social event in fact, but I wish it had not happened.

I was fond of that car. It was a reliable and tough little Honda turbo-diesel and was just right for going around Scotland in all weathers. And it was fast too.

Now it was in a field, a fence post embedded into the front end. A write off. No other cars were involved, so no one to blame or curse, except me.

I was not happy. It was Christmas Eve 2012. I was on my way to London but had only travelled a mile. The weather was foul – very wet and windy and cold. It's often like that in December in Scotland. I should have known better. But I was going too fast. A familiar story.

The empty road was usually ok for fast driving but there was a hidden dip and the road had flooded at that very point, due to the heavy rain. The car was a write off. Luckily for me, I once again escaped without a scratch. But my pride was seriously damaged.

It was starting to look like being a miserable Christmas. I hitched a lift home on the breakdown lorry and made a cup of tea. I was actually quite shaken and upset. Why did I keep doing this? Maybe I'm just a lousy driver and should pack it in and use the buses from now on.

I sat in a chair and made some phone calls. Nobody sounded surprised by my news. I wondered why. My black mood deepened.

But then there came a knock at the door and my pal Jack came in and gave me a masterclass in the bestowing of unconditional positive regard. He brought three things with him – some paracetamol in case I had a headache, the keys to his second car for as long as I needed it and an invitation to dinner.

He had heard of my mishap – in that part of Scotland, they use telepathy as the broadband's so lousy. He was sympathetic and totally non-judgmental.

Besides being a good Samaritan, Jack is a highly insightful counsellor and work colleague, a fellow AA member. He is also a fellow culture enthusiast and we had recently been in Glasgow to see Beckett's Waiting for Godot performed at the Citizens Theatre.

Jack changed my mood and I started feeling quite cheerful again. I have never forgotten that day. They say that you may easily forget the things that people say and do but you will not forget the way they make you feel. It's true, I have never forgotten.

I learnt a lesson that day. That good things come from bad and that every disaster is an opportunity. But how on earth can I have experienced four major prangs without so much as a minor abrasion? Answers on a postcard to my guardian angel.

Chapter 43

Flight Into Egypt – Mummies And Tummies

Hail to thee, O Nile! Who manifests thyself over this land, and comes to give life to Egypt! (Papyrus 2500 BC)

Waking on the first morning of a Nile cruise, you feel like little Dorothy: 'something tells me we're not in Kansas anymore'. The sounds, the smells, the humidity and of course the sights, are totally not Kansas nor European either. The crews of most European river cruise ships don't break off to kneel in prayer five times a day, but this is Egypt, and ours does. As we glide slowly and quietly upriver, we pass an endlessly fascinating pageant of daily life taking place along the river banks just yards away: people fishing, ploughing, cooking, shopping, drawing water, gossiping, beating their donkeys, washing themselves, feeding their children, eating and sleeping. It never stops and it provides seamless variety. To me, it is more fascinating than a trip to the Valley of the Kings or the Temple of Hatshepsut.

Margie and I are doing a Nile cruise with Mike and Susie Eagar and loving it. It is December 2008 – shortly before Christmas and the contrast with the false predictable sentimentality of English Yuletide that we left behind at Gatwick, could not be greater.

We flew to Luxor and the cliches started happening – the heat, the sand, the flies and the beggars. Later we would see the vast ruined temples of Karnak and Edo (cue for everyone to quote Ozymandias). Then the extraordinary burial complex that is the Valley of the Kings, The Aswan Dam, and the wonderful

Abu Simbel (by bus escorted by the military in case of terrorist attack).

Ancient Egypt is an instantly recognisable brand and it lives up to all expectations. Who could not be impressed by the massive architecture, the solemn hieroglyphs, the sinister deities with their jackal's heads and crocodile jaws? But in a sense that is its undoing – once you have confirmed to your satisfaction that the real objects, buildings and images live up to the thousand illustrations of them that you have already seen, most tourist activity becomes permanently tinged with a sense of déjà vu. For me, that didn't make our trip any less worthwhile, it just allowed one to marvel at how daily life along the Nile for the common man today was so similar to depictions made roughly three thousand years ago.

Then there are the bugs – not so much the flies and the mozzies, which are fairly well behaved, I'm talking more of the the micro variety, the ones that get in your stomach with dire results for digestion. The dreaded Gyppy tummy. I think the four of us picked it up on a 'free' day in Luxor when we bravely took a local ferry across the Nile to see how the locals lived. It was overall a good experience and we met some nice locals (typically, one even turned out to be an acquaintance of Mike). However, we met their bugs too.

Mummy wrapping competition, Nile cruise,

That night at the onboard fancy dress party, there was grim humour in the competition to turn ourselves into mummies – wrapped up in rolls of toilet paper.

Nevertheless, we survived, returning in mid-December to Gatwick fit, bronzed and ready to talk of Christmas fare and turkey.

I still think of that pre-Christmas jaunt as one of the best and certainly the best value for money holiday that I have ever had.

Chapter 44
A Maker Of Beautiful Books – Stephanie Wolfe Murray

A maker of beautiful books
Lies in a Borders field (McCall Smith)

In 2014, I contracted shingles. I'd never had it before and thought it a bit of a joke, only it wasn't. I had to isolate for several weeks and got really fed up. I was soon physically sound, but I was left with this terrible malaise that was part depression, part tiredness, part fecklessness. I couldn't finish anything. I couldn't start anything either. I was bad tempered and idle.

The one thing I did try to do was meditate, reading from the little AA meditation book each morning. This little black book, called A Day at a Time, has sold millions of copies worldwide and is a great read. But it is limited by its small size and its focus on the AA way of life. Nothing wrong with that of course, but there are those, I thought, who perhaps might want a slightly broader view of things.

Gradually I got to thinking that I could try to produce something better. My idea was to bring in a bit of History: 'on this day in 1066, William the..', plus a wee poem to tickle the soul and a thought to uplift the mind. As I quite literally had nothing better to do, I started writing a daily poetry/history/thought book – one page per day. The three hundred and sixty-five pages plus one for leap year, took me about three months to write. I really enjoyed doing it because I gained a sense of purpose. And a lot of knowledge of poetry and history too. It really was one of the most enjoyable exercises I've ever done.

Having written the thing (at least it was in digital form), I wondered what to do next. I'd already done a fair bit of writing therapeutic stuff for my employers, Castle Craig Hospital and had been helped greatly by my friends, the website managers Rupert Wolfe Murray and Manuela Boghian. I decided to show them what I had done. Amazingly, they were both very keen that it should be published and said they knew just the right person to act as editor – Rupert's mother, Stephanie.

Stephanie Wolfe Murray, 2000

I had met Stephanie briefly before but did not really know her. I certainly had no idea as to what an eminent figure she was in the publishing world. She was undoubtedly the doyenne of Scottish publishing.

This amazing woman cheerfully undertook to help me, a totally unknown and untried writer, for very little reward, because she was always, as I soon learnt, open to helping people. How lucky I was. Her son Rupert, who assembled a memoir after her death: Stephanie Wolfe Murray – A Life In Books, wrote this:

"she was open to my Dad despite convention and her mother's hysteria; she was open to living in the wilderness; she was open to us, her children, until the day she died; she was open to the challenge of publishing (and aid work) and was open to authors and anyone who wanted to work with her, or stay with us."

With so much help and expertise, my book was published in early 2016. It had been a big effort because unlike say, a novel where the narrative runs on from page to page, with this daily meditation book, each page had to be designed separately.

The whole experience was made pleasurable by the cheerful way that Stephanie, Rupert and Manuela all pitched in to help. Little did I know it, but poor Stephanie must have already been suffering dreadfully from the cancer that was to kill her a year later. Yet she cheerfully attended several promotional events to launch the book and remained interested right to the end. She died in the summer of 2017, a very brave, kind and inspiring person.

At the Edinburgh Book Festival of 2017, a very special tribute event to Stephanie was held. Here's a review that I wrote at the time for Edinburgh website 'Reviewsphere':

A large crowd of friends and family filled the Studio theatre to hear an hour of tributes most ably hosted by publisher Jamie Byng, the present Managing Director of Canongate, who described Stephanie as his Mentor and an inspirational figure in his life.

Speakers included Flora Fraser (daughter of Antonia Fraser, whose Anthology of Scottish Love Poems was an early Canongate success); Alan Taylor – founding editor of The Scottish Review of Books and past Booker judge who spoke of friendship in the formative years of Canongate; Alasdair Gray, whose Scottish Book of the Year Award-winning Lanark was published by Stephanie; Mairi Hedderwick who spoke of help, visits and long journeys in her company.
The evening was fittingly brought to an end by Alexander McCall Smith who read out his poem, specially composed for Stephanie: 'A Maker of Beautiful Books'. She could not have been better described.

A maker of beautiful books
Knows exactly what it is that makes
Paper, card, printer's ink,
The raw words of the writer
Into that lovely object
We call a book; understands
The subtle work of fonts,
Of leading, of bindings,
That makes a book something
We wish to hold to ourselves,
To keep and cherish, to read
At times when the soul is in need
Of solace, of insight, and art
That can transform the quotidian
Into the transcendent......
A maker of beautiful books
Lies in a Borders field
With all the hills as watchmen;

But the books she made
Live on, resolute upon their shelves
In a hundred far-flung places,
Their maker's advocates, her legacy,
Her sure and beautiful touch
Upon our troubled world,
Less troubled for her presence,
Surer, for her example,
Of the possibilities of truth and beauty.
(A. McCall Smith).

Chapter 45
No Coward Soul - Margie's Achievements

No coward soul is mine
No trembler in the world's storm-troubled sphere (E Bronte)

After school, Margie became a student nurse at St Bartholomew's Hospital in London which she really enjoyed. This is perhaps not surprising given her father's involvement in the world of medicine. She must have visited many hospitals with him as a child on occasions such as Christmas day when the whole family would visit the wards of the local hospital.

Student Nurse, 1959 (Saga Magazine)

Margie wrote about her student nurse experiences years later, in an article for Saga Magazine which began:

"As a probationer nurse in 1959, I had a lovely navy cape with a red lining. In the field adjoining the training school was a bull. Naturally I wanted to see if bulls were really enraged by red, so I was waving my cape and shouting "Toro!" safely behind the gate when an enraged bellow of "Nurse!" came from behind me. That was my first meeting with Matron, who had come to view the new recruits and was horrified at my lack of decorum."But that wasn't the only incident, as she went on to say later:"It was my first day on a ward when a patient collapsed and was being resuscitated with an electric pump. Matron suddenly spun round from the bed, spotted me and ordered: "nurse, fetch a kidney dish...Run!" I ran, not that I knew what a kidney dish was, tripped over the resuscitator flex as I dashed towards the sluice, pulling its plug out of the wall. The patient lived, but no brownie points for me!"

Anyone who knows Margie can easily visualise the whole thing. Yet I know for sure that Margie would have made a terrific nurse. It was really sad that she developed an allergy to hospital disinfectants and had to cease her training after eighteen months.

Nevertheless, although disappointed, she put herself into secretarial college in London and was soon enjoying the London life of secretarial work and flat sharing in South Kensington, like many others of her age and background. London in the early 1960s was a fun place to work and to live. It was much cheaper than it is today, and the social scene though relatively small, was a great place to meet people and generally socialise. There was always a party somewhere. It was in this London scene in 1964 that she met me.

One of Margie's most admirable achievements was her obtaining of a degree in History of Ideas from the University of Kingston. She was 48 years old at the time of graduation and was a popular and enthusiastic student who must have brought something special to every session she attended. It involved a great deal of reading and writing assignments for a number of years and she had to combine this with motherly duties. Her conversation, however, became erudite and wide-ranging (it had always been entertaining) and her letter writing reached new heights of wit. Here are the last lines of her letter of application (in 1984) to join the degree course:

....If it does lead to something better I will hope that my satisfied working day will lead to greater skills at child-motivation in the evenings. But it could be that all it will lead to is the arch wherethrough gleams the untravelled world – and that will not be so bad a result. Whiskey, (as Hollinshead found on his first trip to Scotland) and knowledge have much in common. "it invigorateth the mind, banisheth the despondency and quickeneth the blood' But I would like a lot more – and dearly hope there are still enough hooks left in my mind on which I may peg the garments on offer. "It is a sad reflection, but a true one that I knew almost as much at eighteen as I do now" (Dr Samuel Johnson).

You, Sirs, must help me refute it.'
Somebody, presumably a member of the University selection panel, has put below in red ink, a very large tick and the words: 'We will!'

Towards the end of her degree course, Margie sent me her thesis to read and comment upon. Entitled 'Bacon: Popper: And the Problem of Induction', it was extremely well constructed, at least to my poor intellect it seemed so. I was awestruck as to how somebody raising three children almost unaided could find the time to master a whole world of ideas, encompassing the work of just about every philosopher from Aristotle to Zeno. I am still awestruck.

Graduate, 1988

In 2002 Margie embarked on a new crusade. Incensed, as were many people, with a decision of the Royal Parks Authority to close Pen Ponds Car Park, at the centre of Richmond Park, thus effectively denying access to a beautiful sector of the park to all but the fittest - those able to walk several miles. She formed an action group, of which she was the chairman, and raised over 20,000 signatures to get the decision quashed. Counsellors and MPs were lobbied and questions were asked in parliament. Margie was at the centre of of it all and did a great job.
The decision was overturned and thousands who enjoy Pen Ponds every year have much to thank her for.

Margie's interests lay in travel, art, and a wide intellectual curiosity for any unusual ideas. But most of all she was interested in people, with her family first and foremost. They say that you can learn a lot about a person by their friends. Margie had many, with several – Thea, Tessa and Tim for example, going far back to her childhood. She is not in any way a bossy or controlling person, but when her children or friends were threatened, she is a major force.

Despite her degree in History of Ideas, she did not torment herself by searching for the big answers, but simply lived her life in a person-centred manner, giving to every stranger she met an inquiring mind and a positive regard, and to her nearest and dearest, an unconditional love. She always seems to me the epitome of a Pilgrim Soul. And as a result, she remains a very much-loved person.

Without a doubt, I would say that Margie's greatest achievement has been to raise three children to a successful and happy adulthood. She managed to do this without the proper support of her husband and bereft of really any great material resources, apart from her own personal contribution of wisdom, humour and unconditional love. These simple words of American poet Raymond Carver were written just before he died in 1992 – they fit Margie perfectly:

And did you get what you wanted from this life, even so?
- I did.
And what did you want?
-To call myself beloved, to feel myself beloved on the earth.

Chapter 46

Old Men Forget - A Shakespearean Finale

By Jove, I am not covetous for gold,
Nor care I who doth feed upon my cost;
It yearns me not if men my garments wear;
Such outward things dwell not in my desires:
But if it be a sin to covet honour,
I am the most offending soul alive (Shakespeare, King Henry V)

I like to think, as Shakespeare puts it, that honour is more important than wealth, yet like Oscar Wilde, I will die without either, because my ideals are not matched by my performance. I have regrettably, done a lot of dishonourable things in my life.

Yet, I no longer have any desire for wealth, and I am in no danger of falling under Andrew Carnegie's famous dictum that "he who dies rich, dies disgraced". But that is small comfort, because I am already "in disgrace with fortune and men's eyes". and likely to remain so.

Take marriage for example; according to most Christian vows, it is an enduring state - for better or worse, richer or poorer, in sickness and in health. After more than fifty years of our marriage, I cannot escape the fact that my contributions have been the 'worse', the 'poorer' and the 'sickness' elements. I haven't given up on it of course, because marriage is a sacred institution. I can't change the past (and some of it I can't even remember - excess drinking does that to you) but I have tried to change myself. Oh dear. It's still work in progress. Shakespeare wasn't too good at marriage either

Yet in this my eightieth year, I feel cheerful, though It's sometimes hard to work out why. On a personal level, Margie is suffering from Alzheimer's and in residential care, our children and their families are all facing huge challenges and I feel long past my sell-by date. The planet's not too well either – world leaders act out the sort of scenario that blokes in pubs only verbalise, a chunk of world population struggles to meet its most basic sustenance needs, universal pestilence rages, yet nations put more effort into war than healthcare. And as for Brexit... What cheer can we find?

A lot of my pals who are still above ground Increasingly speak doom in the style of Shakespeare's dying John of Gaunt - England, that was wont to conquer others, hath made a shameful conquest of itself... and so forth.

Well, we have a battle on our hands for the future of our country and no mistake, but we still have a choice as to how we respond. and I think we must fight for our country and our futures. I favour Henry V over sad old John of Gaunt any day –

And gentlemen in England now abed
shall think themselves accursed they were not here,
And hold their manhoods cheap whiles any speaks
That fought with us upon St Crispin's day!

The glass is half full, not half empty (though it's only mineral water these days, dammit!). Positive actions and words translate into self-belief and achievement because people are affected by what they hear themselves actually saying.

My fellow men and women give me hope because they are decent people who want to do what is right. Not all of them of course, but most. In bad times, all we can sometimes do is respect each other on an individual basis and rely on our inner strength and that of our nearest and dearest – our family and friends.

I cultivate an attitude of gratitude. Hal Marley who died in 2002, was an US Air Force Psychologist specialising in addiction. He was known as Dr Gratitude. He would quote the laws of physics - that two different things cannot occupy the same space at the same time. Thus, a heart filled with gratitude has no room for fear, resentment, anger or hatred. I sometimes consciously follow the simple exercise of filling my heart with gratitude and it helps – the more I try, the less bitter and twisted I seem to become

I think of our five grandchildren today, on the cusp of adulthood, just as Margie's and my parents were one hundred years ago. I wish that I had been a better role model. Regrettably, much of my lifespan (in sharp contrast to Margie's), reads as a 'chronicle of wasted time' or worse. Perhaps they can learn from my mistakes. I hope so.

Our special youngsters today - Alfie, Ben, Olivia, Oscar and Sophie - have big challenges to face. So did Stanford, Ursula, Ronnie and Mary in their time. The world is always in some kind of state of crisis, be it now, 1920 or when Shakespeare was a teenager. But life should be lived to the full: The time of life is short; to spend that shortness basely were too long.

I say the same words I said before: trust in God, do what's right and always hope for the best, but plan for the unexpected. Whatever happens is likely to surprise you.

PART TWO

ANCESTRY NOTES

Of Mules And Men – A Summary Of Burn Ancestry

A mule has neither pride of ancestry nor hope of posterity, yet it gets on with things (Anon)

A mule, as you doubtless know, is a product of two separate species - the horse and the donkey. It tends to be looked down upon, but it generally leads a useful and blameless life.

If you go back far enough, we're all mules - products of Homo Sapiens and Neanderthals who were interbreeding roughly fifty thousand years ago. Like mules, we mostly lead useful and blameless lives.

Does it matter? Not to me, but perhaps I'm too Neanderthal to worry. What does seem to matter greatly to some people, is the 'quality' of their lineage over the past one thousand years - the period when history started to be properly recorded.

Thus, they will go to great lengths to trace their 'roots'. Discovering even a tenuous link to the aristocracy or even better, royalty in one's family tree can be as thrilling to Mr and Mrs Dull as winning the lottery. This despite the fact that members of the aristocracy, unlike mules, often lead lives that are neither useful or blameless (all my relations excepted, of course).

That said, I have gone through the root-tracing process myself, because a work of this type has to include information on our family's origins, if only as a record for future generations. The following pages contain the results of my research and feedback from a number of family members. I regret that there are some gaps in the data, but the reader may be relieved, as it makes for fewer pages.

Almost every family is a seething cauldron of genes and the Burns are no different. Gene diversity is healthy and any attempt at gene restriction can have negative outcomes (so, no Hapsburg jaws among our lot). However, to those seeking to know their ancestry, this diversity can be bewildering.

Here then is my attempt to summarise the main aspects of the Burn lineage. It won't take long. Afterwards, I discuss each of the main (or most interesting) strands in more detail.

Some of these strands are extremely ancient, going back to Norman times, some highlight success and endeavour in the nineteenth century, and some may be traceable back to the Stuart monarchs who ruled the British Isles in the seventeenth century. There is also evidence of worthy yeoman stock from England, Ireland and Scotland including arch-peasant Wat Tyler, leader of the 1381 Peasants Revolt, duly slain for his efforts. There is talk too, of involvement with the Empress Eugenie, wife of Napoleon III, last Emperor of France. The children of Margie and Christopher and any subsequent issue will contain to some extent, a part of all these genes.

The marriage of Margie Reid and Christopher Burn in 1966 combined four main sets of genes, though there are of course many others. The most notable ones are as follows:

The Russells: from a Norman family that came over with the 1066 conquest, Robert de Roussel accompanied Richard de Clare, Earl of Pembroke (known as Strongbow), in the twelfth-century invasion of Ireland, for which he was later granted lands in County Down around Killough. The family were later created Barons of Killough. Through the succeeding centuries, the family fortunes waned and waxed as they, like many others, were forced to take sides in the religious wars and upheavals that followed.

My great grandfather, Charles Russell, son of Arthur Russell, a cadet of the Russells of Killough, was born at Newry in County Down in 1832. He trained as a lawyer and lived in England where he became Lord Chief Justice and was created Baron Russell of Killowen in 1894. The family home at Killowen, on

Carlingford Lough in County Down, is where he grew up. He was the first man to be created a Life Peer (at his own request), not wishing to give any of his nine children any special treatment over the succession. In fact, members of the subsequent two generations were made life peers, in their own right.

Lt Col The Hon Bertrand J Russell, DSO

His youngest son, my grandfather - Lt. Colonel the Hon Bertrand Russell, was a distinguished soldier and successful businessman whose second daughter was my mother, Ursula. Following Ursula's early death in 1942, his eldest daughter Prudence, became my guardian.

The Burns and Bunns: my father Stanford changed his name from Bunn to Burn in 1933. When reporting for duty as a newly commissioned army Lieutenant, he noticed his commanding officer's poorly concealed amusement at hearing his name, and apparently thought that a change would enhance his chances of promotion.

Harry Hunter Bunn, 1926

Stanford was the son of Harry Hunter Bunn, scion of a Yorkshire family who emigrated to South Africa in 1876. Harry was for many years a Magistrate in the Transkei and fathered fourteen children in the course of two marriages.
Stanford, his eldest son from his second marriage, was educated in England and joined the British army where he rose to the rank of Major in the Royal Scots, before his untimely death in Hong Kong in 1941, at the time of the Japanese invasion.

The Stuarts: Mary Stuart, Margie's mother, was the eldest daughter of the marriage of Elinor Mary Chaytor and Percy Watt Stuart, whose family originated in Garstang, Lancashire.

Percy Watt Stuart, 1913

Her granddaughter Charlotte Stirling (née Eagar), who once gave me an exploding cigar for Christmas, has produced another cracker by tracing the Stuart line back to the royal blood of Charles Edward, the Young Pretender and his mistress (later claiming to be recognised as wife under Scottish law), Clementina Walkinshaw. Charlotte has been tracing her roots for some time and this sensational discovery is still work in progress and not fully proven. Nevertheless, it puts a new gloss on a mother in law whom I had learned to respect but had never thought to treat as royalty.

Mary Stuart and her younger sisters Beatrice and Margaret were born in New Zealand but educated and brought up in England. Their mother was a Chaytor, a family with extensive farming interests in New Zealand then and now.

George Reid, 1902

The Reids: Margie's father, Ronnie Reid was an eminent surgeon as well as a keen amateur painter, fly fisherman, golfer and collector of antiques. He married Mary Stuart In 1929 and they had five children. They divorced in 1959 and he later married Olive Reid who had twin sons by a previous marriage.

Ronnie Reid's Scottish parents George Reid and Helen (nèe Lorimer) left Scotland towards the end of the nineteenth century and set up in business in Salisbury, where they had three children, Ronnie being the youngest. He went to Brighton College before studying medicine at St Thomas's Hospital, London.

Ronnie went to Colchester General Hospital, Essex after qualifying as a doctor and surgeon and transformed it into a centre of medical excellence. All his five children were born there. He died there too, at the surprisingly early age of sixty two.

Four more sets of genes come into the family through our respective grandmothers – Chaytor, Tyler, Leeming and Lorimer.

The Chaytors: Margie's mother Mary Stuart Reid was born Elinor Mary Stuart. Her mother Elinor Mary Chaytor had married Percy Watt Stuart. The Chaytors are an old English family, who came to prominence in the reign of Queen Elizabeth the First.

In 1546 Christopher Chaytor married the daughter of an ancient and illustrious family, the Clervaux, who had come over with William the Conqueror in 1066. This gave the Chaytors great standing and additional lands including Croft, the family seat in North Yorkshire.

Subsequently, several younger sons established themselves in New Zealand where they built up large farming interests which still exist today. Most notable was John Chaytor, grandfather of Margie's mother Eleanor Mary Stuart (Reid).

The Tylers: my Paternal Grandmother was named Aileen Clara Margaret Tyler, one of an established family of South African settlers of British/Irish descent. Aileen's family, who owned a sizeable timber business in Cape Town, claim kinship to the famous Wat Tyler, the Kentish leader of the Peasants Revolt in 1381. I have been unable to trace the lineage, but her family were apparently vehement that this was the case and have in fact campaigned for recognition of Wat Tyler as a leading figure in the cause of democracy.

The Leemings: my maternal grandmother was Dorothy Leeming, of a notable Catholic family of mill owners from the Lancashire area. She was born in Kensington in 1878 and died in 1921. Her father was John George Leeming, a London resident. The Leemings are recorded in the 1861 census as living in Richmond and later in Kensington. Dorothy's mother was Caroline Galassi Cumming, of London. The Galassi's originated in Italy but had mdlived in Soho for several generations.

The Lorimers: Margie's paternal grandmother was Helen Lorimer. They are a highly respected Lowland Scots family, linked through marriage to other notable families such as Sir John Moore (Peninsular War General) and Eugenie, Empress of France. Ancestors could also claim friendship with Robert Burns and Annie Laurie of Maxwellton.

I have recorded below what has come to light so far about the Russells, Burns, Reids, Stuarts, and in lesser detail, the Leemings, Tylers, Chaytors and Lorimers.

In summary, these families can claim distant links respectively to: a Lord Chief Justice of England, a South African Magistrate, A Lowland Scottish family, Bonnie Prince Charlie, a Liverpool merchant, Wat Tyler, Norman conquerors and the Empress Eugenie of France. A fairly representative mix I suppose, whatever that means. Who knows what further research might reveal? There has for example, been at least one mass murderer in the USA named Russell, and another named Reid....

Ancestry Notes 1 - The Russells

My mother Ursula was a Russell, a distinguished family both then and now.

They are a Norman family (originally de Roussel or de Rosel) that came over with the Conqueror in 1066. A few years later, Robert de Roussel accompanied Richard de Clare, Earl of Pembroke (known as Strongbow), in the twelfth-century invasion of Ireland, for which he was granted lands in County Down around Killough. The family were subsequently created Barons of Killough. Through the succeeding centuries, the family fortunes (they were staunch Catholics) fluctuated mightily during the religious wars that bedevilled Ireland for so long. The Papist Russells encountered problems in the Cromwell years. The story goes that Mary Russell, wife of Patrick Russell, had walked from Holyhead to London to petition King Charles II after the Restoration of the Stuart monarchy in 1660, for the return of lands seized by Cromwell. The gallant King had been so impressed that he complied with her request. Of course later, in the aftermath the Boyne in 1690, they had even bigger problems to deal with.

By the start of the nineteenth century, the family was in only moderate circumstances – the seventeenth and eighteenth centuries had not been kind to them overall, though they had been fortunate to keep at least a part of their wealth and reputation. George Russell, a corn merchant in Killough, Co Down, died in 1828 and among his children was Arthur Russell who was for several years a sea captain until marrying Margaret Hamill (née Mullin), a wealthy widow, in 1825. At this, he decided to buy himself a brewery in Newry and settle down. He sounds like a sensible sort of chap. He must have bestowed his wisdom on at least one of his children, because his son Charles Russell (my great grandfather) was to become the family's most illustrious member.

Arthur Russell having died in 1845, the care of his large family devolved upon their talented mother and their paternal uncle. Charles was one of six children, his four sisters all becoming nuns and his brother Matthew was ordained as a Jesuit priest.

Lord Russell of Killowen

Charles Arthur Russell, Baron Russell of Killowen, GCMG, PC was an Irish statesman of the 19th century, and Lord Chief Justice of England. He was the first Roman Catholic to serve as Lord Chief Justice since the Reformation. It is almost impossible to read anywhere a bad word about him, which is impressive and makes him a great role model for future generations.

For further reading, there is The Life of Lord Russell of Killowen by Barry O'Brien that contains some nice stories, though it is 'written by an idiot' (as my grandfather used to say of it). The family, who had commissioned the life, hated the finished version because Barry O'Brien, the author wrote it as if he and Russell were great friends, whereas they were nothing of the kind.

He was a member of Parliament as a Liberal between 1880 and 1894 and then served in the House of Lords as Lord Chief Justice, from 1894 until his death in 1900. Russell was created a life peer at his own request because with nine children, he did not want to single out any one of them for special treatment when it came to inheriting a title. This was a highly unusual arrangement at the time. Modern life peerages were instituted in 1958.

Since then, the barony of Killowen has been created two more times for successive members of the Russell family who have earned a peerage through their own merit.

Russell married Ellen Mulholland, daughter of a Belfast doctor and a childhood friend, in 1858. She bore him ten children and died in 1918.

Admitted a solicitor in 1854, he practised in the county courts of Down and Antrim and became at once the champion of the Catholics who had resisted organised attempts at proselytising by Protestants in these counties. He matriculated at Trinity College, Dublin in 1856, but never graduated. Migrating to Liverpool, he practised as a solicitor and later as a barrister, becoming an MP.

There were many tributes paid to first Baron Russell of Killowen at the time of his death. The English and American Bar Associations and people of the most diverse political and religious views were unanimous in saying that, besides his masterful character as lawyer, judge, and parliamentarian, and his stalwart loyalty to his faith and country, he had enjoyed a rare popularity with all who met him. "In him were blended many qualities not usually found together. With a keen and orderly mind, a resolute will, great capacity for work, and severe official dignity, he combined sensibility of temperament, a spirit of helpfulness and comradeship, and a dreamer's devotion to ideals. He was always ready to write and speak for educational, religious, and benevolent purposes, though such action was not calculated to forward his political ambitions. Devoted to his family, he crossed the continent on his first American trip to visit Mother Mary Baptist Russell of San Francisco (who, with two others of his sisters, had entered the Order of Mercy), and found time to write for his children and send them day by day an admirable account of his experiences." (Wikipedia).

This extract from the Encyclopedia Britannica describes the kind of person he was:

"In private as in public life Russell was always strenuous, and most attracted by things that called for the exercise of activity, whether bodily or intellectual. Inaction he disliked both for himself and in others. Though not an athlete, he took an interest in manly pastimes: he was fond of riding and of breeding horses; he liked being on the racecourse; and he enjoyed games, both of skill and of chance. A student of books he was not; he could lay no claim to wide learning or elegant scholarship; but he could appreciate a good book; he was versed in Shakespeare; and he knew and loved the poetry and the songs of his native land. When he wrote, his style, inornate, clear and forcible, reflected the character of his thought. He was a staunch and sympathetic friend, ever ready, in an unostentatious way, to help, where help was really needed. "

Russell lived at Tadworth Court, near Epsom and was a keen racing man. He owned several horses himself though none were spectacular. He was also a friend of Lord Rosebery whose racing stables were nearby at The Durdans. Rosebery was Prime Minister when he won the Derby in successive years and Russell was there to see it happen. During his term as prime minister, Rosebery won several races besides the Derby. His horses often ran in Russell's racing colours because it was deemed unsuitable at the time for a prime minister to engage in such trivial pursuits as horse racing (but apparently OK for a judge to do so).

I think of Russell and Rosebery quite often these days, because Annabel keeps her horse in stables next to the Durdans. I sometimes go to watch her ride in the magnificent indoor school, next to the house where Rosebery died in 1929, listening to the strains of the Eton Boating Song, his final request.

Russell's knowledge of racing was immense. At an Ascot meeting, an ambassador's wife asked him to give her a good tip. Russell did so and the horse won, and the lady delightedly exclaimed 'what a first class judge you would make', to which Russell replied: 'tell that to the Lord Chancellor'.

Sir Charles Russell, Epsom 1890

There is also the story of a wealthy American, sharing a first-class compartment on an overnight train from Paris to the South of France. His fellow-traveller was an amiable gentleman. On the journey they played poker, so as to pass the time. The gentleman proceeded to relieve him of a goodly though not enormous, sum of money. On arrival at Nice, he departed giving the American his card and saying he hoped they would meet again. The man, thinking he had been duped by a professional gambler, was astonished to read on the card the name 'Sir Charles Russell'.

Russell's children would play poker with him before bedtime but when they woke in the morning, the money they lost was always there beside their beds.

In Ireland a couple of years ago, I went to the town hall in Newry, County Down which is near the small village of Killowen where Charles Russell was born and lived his early years. There is a large statue of him in the entrance, as so there should be. I took a photograph.

Lord Russell Statue, Newry, 2016

As barrister and later as judge, his courtrooms were always a sell-out with the public seeking entertainment. His ready wit and sense of drama were legendary. Here is an exchange taken from 'The Life of Lord Russell of Killowen':

He was once questioning a witness called Sampson:

'Did you hear my question?' he asked him gently.
' I did', replied Sampson.
'Did you understand it?' asked Russell even more gently.
'I did'. Said the witness
'Then why have you not answered it?' Shouted Russell in a voice like thunder, 'Tell the jury why you have not answered it!'

Russell is also credited with this little courtroom gem:

Barrister: 'What would be the highest penalty for bigamy, M'lud?
Judge (Russell): 'Two mothers in law'.

Really, the man should have had a career on the stage.

The Russells lived at Tadworth Court, on the edge of Epsom Downs. It is now a childrens' home. Sir Charles Russell is buried as he wished, in the family plot at Epsom on the hill below the racecourse, within the sound of the horses' hooves.

Sir Charles Russell fathered ten children (the eldest, Lillian was to live only five years):

Lillian Frances (b.1859 d.1864)

Arthur Joseph Russell, Barrister and County Court Judge (b.1861), married Florence Cuming.

Honourable Sir Charles Russell, 1st Baronet, KCVO (1863-1928) (created a Baronet in 1916)

Honourable Eileen Mary Russell (b.1865), married Douglas Lyon Holms

Honourable Cyril Russell (b.1866), whose son Alec Charles Russell (1894-1934) inherited his uncle's baronetcy, by special reminder.

Francis Xavier Joseph Russell (1867-1946), who would in 1929 be created Baron Russell of Killowen

Honourable Mary Gertrude Russell (b.1874) a nun

Honourable Lilian Russell (b. 1878), married Henry Olpherts Drummond.

Honourable Margaret Russell (b. 1879)

Bertrand Russell 1878-1960

My grandfather Bertrand Russell, (whose second eldest daughter Ursula was my mother) was the youngest of the Russell boys and more details of his life and times are to be found in Chapters 8 to 10. There were four daughters: Prudence, Ursula, Joan and Clodagh. Below is an extract from the Epsom and Ewell history Explorer:

After his schooling, eighth-born Bertrand Joseph went into the Army, joining the Royal Horse Artillery. He fought in South Africa during the Boer War, taking part in actions west of Pretoria in July 1900, for which he was awarded the Queen's Medal with three clasps.

Of slight build (unlike his burly father), he was an excellent horseman and rode in point to points and other events on his own horses. He was also very keen on racing and owned several racehorses.

The young lieutenant returning from the South African war must have seemed quite a hero. He seems to have quickly re-entered London life.

In 1902, he married Dorothy Leeming (known as Dolly), who was the daughter of John Leeming, a wealthy Londoner, from a well-known Catholic family with roots in the North of England.

When Bertrand Russell married Dorothy in 1902, she would have been aged 24, and presumably had inherited part of her parents' estate.

Holt Manor, Trowbridge, Wiltshire

They lived in Wiltshire for a while, near to the army complex around Salisbury plain. The 1911 Census records Bertrand ("Captain, Royal Horse Artillery") and Dorothy visiting his brother Cyril and family in their grand Kensington House in Bayswater. However, their family home was The Manor House, Holt, Nr Trowbridge, Wiltshire and the Census records the couple's three young children (a fourth was born in 1912) there together with eight domestic servants.

In 1906, Bertrand was appointed Aide de Camp to the Viceroy of Ireland, Lord Aberdeen and the couple lived at Dublin castle and enjoyed the Irish social and sporting scene.

The War of 1914-18 ended this golden age, and Bertrand was sent to France and was soon in action.

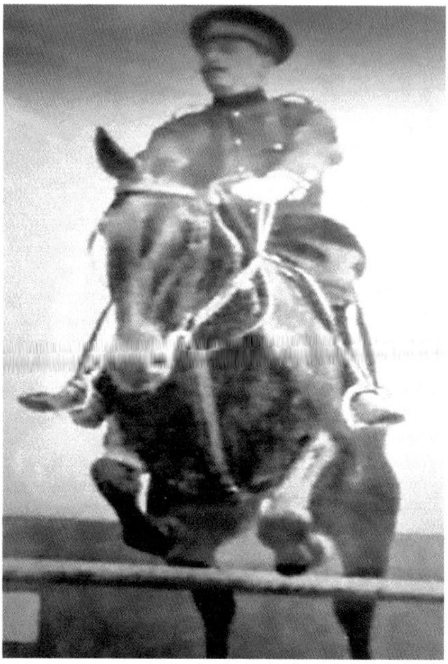
Captain Russell on 'Jack', Dublin Horse Show, 1906

He was wounded on one occasion in 1914 meriting a "Mention in Dispatches". He was twice wounded again on 9 May 1915, displaying bravery for which he was awarded the

Distinguished Service Order. The citation in the London Gazette is: "The Honourable Bertrand Joseph Russell, Capt. (Reserve of Officers), 104th Battery, Royal Field Artillery. On 9 May 1915, near Rue Petillon (Fromelles), this officer commanded a section in the trenches, greatly helping the infantry. He was heavily shelled all day, the parapet in front of one gun being destroyed. They kept on firing, however, and the success was greatly due to the courage displayed by Capt Russell, who was twice wounded earlier in the day."
He was later promoted and transferred to the Italian front, where he earned himself the Italian Croix de Guerre.

Meanwhile, his wife Dorothy was showing spirit too, by doing war work in France herself. She spent a year at Etaples, near Calais at the main Reinforcement Camp for the British Army. Here troops in transit from England could train before going up to the line, and troops also came from the line to rest there. Dolly worked as a volunteer with a Catholic group providing a canteen as well as social and spiritual support. There was no NAAFI in those days. When back in London, she did similar work near Victoria Station.

When Dorothy died of multiple sclerosis in 1921, at the early age of 44, leaving four young daughters, her rapid decline was put down partly to her exhausted state due to her war work. Bertrand had to make changes and moved back to London

Dorothy Russell (Leeming) 1915

Bertrand remarried in 1922 to Mavis Hazell of Frinton on Sea, Essex. she was considerably younger than him and this marriage was probably not popular with the four Russell daughters. there was one son of their marriage: Michael, born in 1923 - he served in the RAF in the war and later lived in Kenya where he was a pilot for East African Airways. Michael was twice married and had four children - Christopher and Julia by his first wife Jean, and Anna and Verena by his second wife, Judy. They moved back to the UK around 1970 and lived in East Grinstead, Surrey. Michael died in 1993.

Unfortunately, the marriage was not a success. Mavis was diagnosed with some kind of mental illness, possibly schizophrenia, and spent many years in a mental institution. I believe that she died about 1956. Bertrand and Mavis divorced in 1936.

Some time in the late 1920's, Bertie entered the world of business. He had met a young American chemist named Albert Fishburn who had developed a new formula for printing ink and in 1929 backed him financially to start his own business – The Fishburn Printing Ink Company Ltd., of Watford. Bertie became Chairman. This soon became a very successful and profitable business and Bertie remained involved until the War ended in 1945. When Albert Fishburn retired in 1964, the business was sold to an American company.

At about the same time, his other great interest was the breeding and showing of Shetland sheepdogs, in which he achieved much success breeding several champions. He and his housekeeper May would travel the country to attend shows and became well known figures. An obituary in the breed's magazine following his death in 1960 concluded: "It is such men as he whom we need so much in the dog world".

Bertie's first wife, Dorothy (Dolly) was a much-loved person whose place in the family was sadly never filled. The four Russell girls however, rallied to support each other and their father in a way that would have made Dolly proud.

At a 2011 dinner attended by over eighty descendants of Sir Charles Russell, a summary of the Prudence, Ursula, Joan, Clodagh's lives and their half-brother Michael as well, was part of the supporting programme (see below). Such admirable people.

Bertie's Children

As Presented at the Russell Reunion Dinner for the Descendants of Lord Russell of Killowen

25th March 2011, Chartered Accountants Hall, Moorgate Place, London.

Prudence, the eldest, born in 1904 with a brief stage career and a failed childless marriage behind her, stepped bravely into the breach following the wartime deaths of Ursula and her husband, Stanford Burn. She adopted their four children, Jancis (12), Lucinda (6), Caroline (4) and Christopher (2). She raised the children at her home near Harrogate. The girls were educated at Mayfield and St Leonard's, Christopher at Ampleforth. In 1952 she made a happy second marriage with Gordon Findlay. She and Gordon lived in Yorkshire, at Spofforth, apart from a period in Malta after Gordon retired. Prue died in 1978 and Gordon in 1981.

Ursula, born on 1905, married Stanford Burn of the Royal Scots in 1929 (who later changed the family name to Burn). In the 1930's the regiment was in India but when war came, it formed part of the Hong Kong garrison, with Stanford as Second in Command. Hong Kong fell to the Japanese on Christmas Day, 1941, a week or so after Stanford was killed in one of the enemy's early assaults. Ursine and her children were in the safety of Ootacamund in Southern India when she fell sick and she too died the following May.

Joan, born 1908, went from Mayfield to Oxford (she used to lament in later life that she was 'brainy' at school when she would far rather have been 'sporty') and then to work in London. In 1933 she married Charles Brand, a civil engineer from a Scottish Catholic family, whose sisters had been at school with her. Charles' firm, originally founded by his great-grandfather, built tunnels and harbour works: he was made CBE in 1963 after completing the road tunnel beneath the Clyde in Glasgow. They lived in South Kensington, with a seaside cottage on the Solent, where Charles sailed small boats off the beach. Andrew was born in 1937, Duncan in 9141 and Felicity in 1945. Boys followed Charles to Stonyhurst, Felicity her mother to Mayfield. Charles died, aged only 60, in 1966, Joan in 1997.

Clodagh, born 1912, 'finished' in Paris after Mayfield, then studied piano in Munich. In 1936 she was visiting her sister Ursula in the Indian hill station used in summer by the Royal Scots, and there met Tommy Haddon, a young officer of the Border Regiment. Three years later they married in England, days after the outbreak of war, just before Tommy crossed to France with the BEF. After Dunkirk, Tommy divided his his wartime between regimental service (he took part in the Allied landings in Sicily and Italy) and staff jobs, including a spell at the Cabinet Office in the Whitehall bunkers; in this way, he and Clo managed some family life in either London or Camberley. In 1944, Tommy commanded his regiment in the airborne assault on Arnhem, where he was taken prisoner of war. Or son, Paul, had been born in 1940, Martin followed in 1944 and John in 1947. In the Russell tradition, the boys all went to Beaumont. Tommy had a variety of jobs post-war, including big roles in Singapore, Hong Kong and Whitehall, being made CBE and retiring as Brigadier in 1968. He and Clo lived near Hindhead in Surrey. He died in 1993, she in 1999, the survivor of her generation.

Michael, born 1923, joined the wartime RAF on leaving Beaumont, got his wings, but too late in the war to see combat. On leaving the Air Force, he worked as a pilot in Burma, Hong Kong and Africa. In 1949 he married Jean Cannon from Rangoon, and they settled in Nairobi. Christopher was born in 1951 and Julia in 1954. There was a divorce in 1959. Michael later married Judy Roberts of Kenya. Anna Katherine was born in1961 and Verena in 1962. In time, the family moved to England, settling in the vicinity of Gatwick, from where he flew for a variety of airlines. He retained the family interest in horses and racing, as did his sisters. He was just 70 when he died in 1998. He was the youngest child of the youngest son of Lord Chief Justice Russell.

Ancestry Notes 2 – The Bunns and Burns

The Bunn's (my father Stanford was the only one of fourteen siblings to change his name to Burn) are originally a very English family. The name apparently came into use after the Norman conquest of 1066 to mean a person of good character, originating from the French word 'bon'. My Grandfather Harry Hunter Bunn, who I never met, seems to have been the most notable in recent history. He emigrated to South Africa in about 1876, becoming a magistrate in the Transkei, and fathering 14 children with two wives.

Harry Hunter Bunn was born in 1859, in Tosside near the town of Settle, in Yorkshire, to Henry Bunn and Isabella Bunn (born Hunter).

His father, Henry had been born in 1812, in Worcester, and is recorded as being a curate at Calne Church, Wiltshire and later a schoolmaster and vicar at Tosside. He appears to have been the son of Joseph Bunn and his wife Ann (nee Parry) of Worcester. Henry died in Settle in 1864. He must have made a success of the remote parish because he was apparently appointed bishop designate of Ripon, when unfortunately illness befell him and he died (this is according to the account of his grandson, Peter Bunn). Isabella was born circa 1821, in Keswick, Cumberland. She died in 1875 in Scarborough.

Harry had three siblings. He was educated first (briefly) at Giggleswick, near Settle, a minor public school at the time, where his school entry reads: "Bunn, Harry Hunter. Son of Mrs Bunn, Stackhouse, Settle. Left Christmas, 1868. Resident Magistrate Libode, Pondoland West; J.P. for Cape Colony. Served in Frontier Mounted Police..." He thereafter went to St Edmund's school, Canterbury, presumably because it had special arrangements for taking the impoverished children of clergy and his father Henry, a vicar, had died in 1864.

Tosside, birthplace of Harry Hunter Bunn

Harry Hunter Bunn was a man of his time. He seems to have been the sort who, if he did not actually build the British Empire, most certainly worked a lifetime at strengthening it. Born in 1859 in Yorkshire, he went to South Africa in 1876 when he would have been just 17 years old, and apparently returned to Britain on occasional visits, as when his children attended English schools. He joined the Cape Mounted Police, later becoming a magistrate in the Transkei in 1880, work which he continued until retiring in 1906.

Harry H Bunn, Cape Mounted Police, 1900

Harry had two wives and produced seven children with his first wife, Sarah Annie Bennett (married 1880) – Henry, Clarence, Isabel, Herbert, Tamplyn, Lionel and Maud.

He married his second wife, Aileen Clara Margaret Tyler in 1903. She was born in 1882 and would have been 21 at the time of the wedding - 23 years younger than Harry. Together they had a further seven children – Stanford (my father), Henry, Charles, Arthur, Cecil, Eileen, Peter.

Aileen lived until 1967. Following the death of Harry in 1926, at some stage she returned to the UK and the 1939 census records her living in England at Birds Cottage, Dunmow, Essex, England. This would probably have been because some of the children were being educated in England. She died in South Africa in 1967.

Jean Coulter, a South African writer whose maiden name was Bunn (she is the daughter of Lionel Bunn, son of Harry Hunter Bunn), has written books about life during her childhood in the Transkei: she said. " In those days there was little entertainment and storytelling, or 'yarning' as we called it, was a great pastime. Being a teenager in those years was nothing like being a teenager today."

Harry was said to be very good at yarning. However, he does not appear to have been very good at business. In his later years it seems that he invested a large part of his savings in a South African coal mine which proved unproductive, bringing him to the verge of bankruptcy. At this point, he began studies to become a Church minister.

Harry's children took up a number of different occupations including Postmaster, Magistrate, General Trader and Policeman. At least two of his children – Stanford and Peter, were educated in England at St Edmund's School, Canterbury and later joined the British army. Both Harry himself and his brother John had been educated at St Edmund's in earlier years.

My father, Major Stanford Burn was born in 1904 in South Africa, the eldest son of Harry Hunter Bunn and his second wife Aileen. He married Ursula Russell, daughter of Lt.-Col. Bertrand Joseph Russell and Dorothy Leeming, on 1 May 1929. He died in December 1941 at Hong Kong, listed as killed in action. He gained the rank of Major in the Royal Scots. He was given the name of Stanford Bunn at birth. In 1933 his name was legally changed to Stanford Burn by Deed Poll. Stanford was educated at St Edmund's School, Canterbury, England.

He seems to have achieved more on the sporting and OTC side of things than through academic studies.

The following entry in the St Edmund's list of Alumni, plus other sources, was kindly provided by ex-deputy headmaster Jock Asbury-Bailey :

Stanford Bunn, born fourth of March 1904, at St Edmund's School May 1919 to December 1922.

When Stanford arrived at St Edmund's, aged just 15, there were about 150 boys at the school, of whom 100 were clergy orphans, about 30 were in the Junior School (9-13), with the remainder in Senior School (13-18), but by no means all of them went through to the Sixth Form. He was in North House, one of three houses, North, West and East, depending upon which part of the country a boy came from and they were divisions only used for sporting activities.

Hockey was played in 1920 for the first time since 1916. In 1921 he was playing outside right and was awarded his First XI colours, as he was again in 1922.

Cricket. He played one Second XI match, against Wye College, in 1920, scoring 0 and taking 1-6 in bowling. In 1921 he batted number 10 or 11 usually. 13 innings, twice not out, total runs 59, highest score 17*, average 5.3. He was nevertheless awarded his First XI colours.

In 1922 he started batting at no 6, but later opened the innings at no 2 and finished fourth in the batting averages: In a house match against East that year, he opened the innings and scored 78 and 55, although North lost the match by 10 wickets. He was again awarded First XI colours. He did not bowl at all for the First XI.

Football. In 1920 Stanford played in goal against the Old Boys. In 1921 he played in 3 matches for the Second XI, twice in the forwards and once in goal. In 1922 he played for the First XI, in the forwards, and was awarded First XI colours.

Sports (Athletics). He came Third in the Long Jump in 1921 and won the Long Jump with a distance of 17 ft 3 ½ ins in 1922. He was awarded Sports colours.

In the O.T.C. (Officer Training Corps) he passed his Certificate 'A', parts 1 and 2 in 1921 and was appointed Lance Corporal. He was a First class shot. He was promoted to Sergeant in 1922.

He was awarded Lower Sixth Privileges in September 1921 and was appointed a School Monitor in September 1922. Member of the Choir. Second class Swimming Certificate. Left 1922, in the Upper Fifth, having obtained a Cadetship into Sandhurst, at the age of 18 years and 9 months.

Stanford duly went through Sandhurst during 1923-1924. He was commissioned a 2nd Lt. in the Royal Scots in 1924 and saw overseas service in Nigeria, West Africa, India and Hong Kong as well as in the UK.

He was known as a very fine horseman and a leading member of the regimental polo team, an important part of peacetime activities. His brother Peter said that Stanford's love of horses came from the time he spent in England as a schoolboy, staying during school holidays in Norfolk with his mother, where there was a pony and trap and other horses to ride.

Stanford died in the fall if Hong Kong in December 1941 aged 37, as described in detail in the opening chapters of this book.

His wife and my mother, Ursula Burn, nee Russell was born on 28 May 1905, daughter of Lt.-Col. Bertrand Joseph Russell and Dorothy Leeming. She married Stanford, on 1 May 1929. She died of a cerebral haemorrhage in May 1942 at Ootacamund, Tamil Nadu, India.

Ancestry Notes 3 - The Stuarts

Margie's grandmother Elinor Mary Chaytor, married Percy Watt Stuart in 1906, at Marshlands, South Island, New Zealand. Sadly, a few years later, she developed a brain tumor and despite travelling to London for treatment during World War I, she died in New Zealand in 1917, at the young age of 43. Margie's mother, also named Elinor Mary, would have been just 10 years old at the time.

The Chaytors are discussed in a later section. The Stuart ancestry is complicated and surprising, to say the least. A notable seventeenth century figure in the Stuart lineage seems to have been Scottish adventurer and banker Sir William Paterson (1658-1719), though how he comes to be connected (presumably by marriage) to the Stuarts is not clear. He is famous as a founder of the Bank of England and later infamous as the main instigator of the disastrous Darien adventure in Panama, which bankrupted the Scottish government at the end of the seventeenth century, requiring bailout by the English. This eventually led to the Act of Union in 1708.

Percy Watt Stuart, Margie's maternal grandfather, lived in New Zealand for many years, though he was born in England in 1871 and died in a nursing home in Essex in 1948. His line of the Stuart family goes back to Garstang, in Lancashire.

Later generations of Stuarts seem to have retained connections with the Bank of England. Herbert Stuart, Margie's great uncle, became a senior Bank official before being called to serve in the carnage of World War I, from which he never returned.

John and Elinor Chaytor, Percy and Elinor

Herbert's younger brother, Percy Watt Stuart began an unsatisfactory career in the Bank, before then trying stockbroking. Apparently, he would knock off every morning at 11 am and go round to a convivial watering hole like the Jamaica Inn for a glass of champagne and a slice of cake. Something tells me that I would have got on well with the man.

However, Percy soon got bored with the City, telling his father that he 'couldn't stand the life' and thought he would try his luck in the Colonies. He fetched up in Wellington, New Zealand with 15/6p in his pocket and immediately spent half of it on oysters for lunch. He carried with him two things that he considered indispensable to a gentleman in the colonies - a supply of stiff white collars and a butter knife.

He soon fell on his feet and got a job with Dalgety's, the leading pastoral and agricultural company, on the meat buying side. He would go from farm to farm buying cattle and at the end of the drive, would put on his stiff white collar and go up to the front door. One day he went up the Chaytors' drive at Marshlands, their large farming estate and so met his future wife, Elinor Mary. Elinor's father, who had quite a few children, was so pleased to see a man wearing a stiff white collar (and with his own butter knife), not to mention an aristocratic name, that he approved of their romance. They were married in 1906.

There are a number of other stories about him. The butter knife seems to have been quite an obsession. He was a person of the most exacting standards and indeed once thrashed a man for not using a butter knife. "Most unfair as, though it might have been understandable if it happened in some club in St James, this happened at Marshlands when he was lending a hand with mustering sheep. Marshlands was quite large so there were huts scattered about where people could stay while about their duties. One evening the chaps were gathered around the table for supper when one of the men reached out with his pocket knife to get butter. There was a roar of rage from Percy, who bellowed: "Simmonds you beast", and laid about the unfortunate Simmonds with his stockwhip." I am indebted to Tony Lugg, Margie's cousin, and Charlotte Stirling, Margie's niece for these stories about Percy.

Ancestor-tracing is a bit like metal detecting. You spend hours dredging through dross and then suddenly bingo! Pure gold. I had such a moment recently, thanks to Charlotte Stirling (née Eagar) – novelist, film maker and investigative journalist, who has delved into the background of this side of the family in great detail. And she has unearthed a remarkable story.

Her proposition is a link back to the eighteenth century, through Mary (nee Stuart) the wife of Ronnie Reid and mother of Deidre, Sally, Francie, Margie and David – back to Charles Edward Stuart, the Young Pretender to the Throne of Scotland, aka Bonnie Prince Charlie. Royal blood, no less!

So, could there be royal Stuart genes in the DNA of the Burn children? It seems possible. Here is the gist of it:

Through Margie and Francie's mother, Elinor Mary Stuart, there is a line back to Bonnie Prince Charlie and his Scottish mistress (who claimed also to be his wife under Scottish law), Clementina Walkinshaw. This line is said to exist because Charlie and Clementina had a secret child, named Clementina Douglass (Douglass was a common pseudonym used by the Prince), who was kept hidden in the Lake District until her death 21 years later. It is well known that the two had a later daughter, known as Charlotte, Duchess of Albany, but this earlier, secret daughter has only recently been unearthed.

The secret child, Clementina Douglass is said to have had at least one child herself, in the Lake District, before dying in 1771, quite probably in childbirth. The child in this fatal childbirth (a boy) was adopted by a local family named Backhouse (they later called themselves Backhouse Stuart). This is the start of the line that is said to culminate after several generations, in Percy Watt Stuart who married Margie's mother, Elinor Mary Stuart.

This adopted son of Clementina Douglass was known first as Nicholas Backhouse but later as William Stuart.

To recap on the history behind all this: the Stuart kings ruled Britain for most of the seventeenth century until King James II lost his throne in 1688. James retired to exile in France. His son, calling himself James III and known as the Old Pretender, tried to regain his throne in 1715. This attempt, known as the 1715 rebellion, failed and the Old Pretender lived out the rest of his life in exile, first in France, and then in Rome. It was there that his eldest son, Charles Edward Stuart, known as Bonnie Prince Charlie - the Young Pretender - was born in 1720.

The story of the Young Pretender's attempt to reclaim the throne in 1745 (known as the '45 rebellion') is well known. His attempt started promisingly after he arrived back in Scotland and quickly raised support and an army. After winning several battles in Scotland he marched into England as far South as Derby, where tragically, things started to go wrong as his supporters began to get cold feet and left the young prince with no choice but to turn back. From then, it was a matter of just a few months until the final bloodbath at Culloden that put paid to the Jacobite dreams. It had been a good try, but the final outcome was a sad return to exile in Europe, where the shattered Young Pretender descended into depression and alcoholism, dreaming of what might have been. His mistress, Clementina Walkinshaw, whom he reputedly first met at Holyrood House, Edinburgh in 1745, joined him in exile in 1752. By 1760 she had had enough and left him, unable to put up with his drinking and foul moods.

Clementina was publicly linked with Bonnie Prince Charlie for much of their adult lives, from 1746 until his death in 1787, first as his mistress, then as the mother of his acknowledged daughter, Charlotte Stuart. Clementina may well have had an earlier, secret daughter by Bonnie Prince Charlie. Furthermore, she also had a good claim to be legally married to him under Scottish law, which states that a marriage can be legal without a church ceremony, if a couple have been cohabiting by habit and repute and or with intention to marry (such intention being manifested by subsequently having sex). This would be especially the case if she were carrying his child

Did Charlotte, acknowledged daughter of the Young Pretender and Clementine Walkinshaw, have an elder sister, Clementina Johannes Sobiesky Douglass – born in 1746 and a potential strategic bombshell for the Stuarts, who was hidden from babyhood in the remote village of Finsthwaite, near Lake Windermere, until her early death in 1771?

The Finsthwaite churchyard contains the grave of a Clementina Johannes Sobiesky Douglass who is known locally as the 'Finsthwaite Princess'– a child obviously named for Bonnie Prince Charlie's mother Princess Clementina Sobieski, and his great-grandfather, King John Sobiesky of Poland. If the proposition is true, this is one of the Stuarts' best-kept secrets and is still a mystery today. This little girl known as Clementina Douglass, according to local tradition, arrived in the care of a Jacobite officer calling himself James Douglas (no relation), in the late 1740's.

The above facts and conjectures are interesting to scholars of that particular period of history. There does seem however, to be evidence of a link through this mysterious Finsthwaite Princess and her supposed son, Edward Backhouse Stuart, down through several generations to Percy Watt Stuart who is mentioned above. Could Clementina Douglass have done exactly as her sister Charlotte did, ten years later, and taken a secret lover or husband, have a child, possibly two, before dying in childbirth in 1771?

If all this is so, it seems likely that Edward Backhouse Stuart (aka William Stuart) was one of these children, an adopted child who lived in the area and continued this Stuart line?

It is difficult to prove several key facts in all this, especially the following:

- Did Clementina have a child, before the well-documented Charlotte, Duchess of Albany?

There is evidence to support it, such as this diary entry by James Edgar, nephew of James Edgar, who was Secretary of State to James III, the Old Pretender's secretary. London 14th February 1754: "[Clementina Walkinshaw] has got in with the prince, has born him two children and has got an extreme ascendant over him. The King's friends in England are firmly persuaded of this and very uneasy."

- If yes, did this child live at Finsthwaite, as Clementina Douglass and if so, why Finsthwaite?

Apart from local tradition, there is little to support this. The apparent arrival of a Jacobite soldier in the village, escorting a small child in 1746 is no real direct link to either The Young Pretender or Walkinshaw.

- Did Clementina Douglass then have a child herself and if so, was he named Nicholas Backhouse (later William Stuart)?

- There is circumstantial evidence of an unaccounted-for child appearing in the Backhouse family at this time. It could also be a reasonable assumption that Clementina Douglass' death at age 24 was the result of childbirth. But there are other possible conclusions too.

Edinburgh University has conducted DNA tests to identify the Royal Stuart DNA. The University, as part of this programme, tested a daughter of Elinor Mary Reid (nee Stuart) - this was Margie Burn - in 2014, and found a strong DNA link (third cousins), between her and Bonnie Prince Charlie's Polish descendants from Charlotte, Duchess of Albany. The likelihood is that this DNA link comes via Margie's possible descent from Clementina Johannes Sobieski Douglass.

This DNA testing provides the strongest evidence in the whole story. It does seem remarkable that a member of the current Stuart/Reid family who was tested should produce such a strong match to the royal Stuarts. Perhaps we will find a way of progressing this science to get more results.

Apart from the excitement over possible royal blood, this particular branch of Stuarts appears to have been fairly humdrum. The family were originally called 'Backhouse Stuart' but dropped the 'Backhouse' at some point in the nineteenth century.

Percy Watt Stuart's grandmother was Mary Ann Cremer Watt, a sugar heiress from Barbados who eloped with William Backhouse Stuart to marry at Gretna Green in about 1826 (they were both under age). The marriage was apparently a happy one and their son William (Percy Watt's father), went on to marry Elizabeth Miriam Straker, a Londoner who reportedly became the first female member of London County Council.

Another of William Backhouse Stuart and Mary Ann's grandchildren was Elizabeth, who became a well known opera singer and a friend of the Swedish diva Jenny Lind. Yet another sibling was Mary, who married Frank Hankinson, Mayor of Coventry in the early part of the twentieth century.

Ancestry Notes 4 - The Reids

Now for the Reid family, which originates in Dumfrieshire – part of that region of South West Scotland known as Galloway. Reid is an old Scottish name meaning 'Red' in relation to hair colour - an attribute of Margie and several of her family. The Reids are a sept of the clan Robertson.

Ronnie Reid with Margie, July 30th 1966

Margie's father Ronnie Reid was the elder son of Scottish parents, George and Helen Reid, who came South from Scotland in the late nineteenth century and set up in business in Salisbury. Ronnie had one elder sister Margaret, known as Peggy and a younger brother Alexander, known as Alec. I cannot find much record of George's forebears. Helen's family name was Lorimer. Many Reids and Lorimers lived around the little town of Moniaive, in the Dumfries and Galloway area. Little is known about George and Helen's time in Salisbury. Around the year 1900, Kelly's Directory lists them at 46 Devizes

Road, Salisbury, Wiltshire - 'George Reid, Travelling Draper'.

Ronnie and his siblings, Peggy and Alec, grew up in Salisbury and went to the local primary schools. They seem to have lived a settled existence at 46 Devizes Road.

Peggy, Ronnie, Alec ,and their mother at Devizes Road, Salisbury, 1910

Peggy, Ronnie and Alec with their mother

The 1911 Census describes their household in the class-conscious terminology of the day:

Household
Head - George Reid 35
Wife - Helen Reid 39
Daughter - Margaret Reid 7
Son - Ronald Reid 5
Son - Alexander Reid 1
Servant - Alice Abel 21

Ronnie Reid was a bright lad and went on a scholarship to Brighton College as a boarder, where he must have done well, although according to the College, he was only a pupil there from September 1921 to April 1922.

Ronnie Reid, Brighton College, 1921

However, the education he received must have been considerable because his later medical studies showed him as a gifted student who won many prizes.

He is recorded as being in Walpole House, a separate house in the town which is no longer a part of the College. The conditions there seem to have been rather basic and crowded, according to some old photographs kindly supplied from archives

The dormitory has beds very similar to the ones that I slept in at Ampleforth.

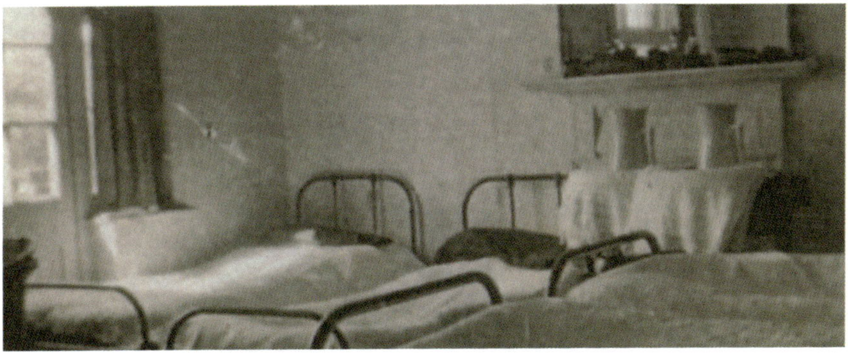

Dormitory, Brighton College, 1921

In 1923, Ronnie enrolled at St Thomas's Hospital Medical School, London where his progress was stellar.

He married Elinor Mary Stuart in 1929 and by 1930, when he was still only 24 years old, he was qualified and ready to embark on his lifetime work as a surgeon. He started at Colchester General Hospital where he soon became a consultant and was instrumental in making it a leading centre for medicine in the country.

After the war, with the coming of the NHS, he remained involved and sat on various committees of governance as well as continuing his work as a surgeon.

Ronnie and Mary divorced in 1960. It was clearly, a difficult time for the family. However, Ronnie met and married in 1961, Olive Gates, the widow of an RAF officer who had twin teenage sons, John and Raphael. Olive and her children integrated well and Ronnie and Olive lived contentedly in Dedham, Essex for several years until his untimely death in 1968.

Mary meanwhile, spent time in Wales, Scotland and Dorset until eventually finding happiness with Ronald Morris, a kindly retired Glasgow solicitor. They lived at Kilmacolm, Renfrewshire for some years before Mary sadly suffered a stroke in 1977, which incapacitated her. However, Ronald continued to care for her with great kindness until she died in 1978. Ronald Morris continued to live at Kilmacolm and died a few years later.

Ronnie Reid was semi-retired when he died in 1968, aged just 62. It was a great shock. Here is his obituary, as published by the Royal College of Surgeons:

Reid, Ronald William (1906 - 1968)

Occupation: General Surgeon.Titles/Qualifications: MRCS 1928, FRCS 1931, MB BS London 1928, MS 1929, LRCP 1928

Born on 4 January 1906 at Salisbury, of Scottish parents, he entered St Thomas's Medical School in 1923 from Brighton College, and distinguished himself consistently throughout his student career, being awarded the Beaney Scholarship and Sutton Sams Prize in 1927. He had an exceptional climax in the years 1928 to 1929: qualifying with the Conjoint Diploma and the degrees of London University and winning the Bristowe Medal in 1928, and passing the examinations for the Final Fellowship and for the MS degree at the age of 23 in 1929; he was also proxime accessit for the coveted Cheselden Medal in surgery, as runner-up to H Hamilton Stewart. All this he achieved without any obvious effort, while he lived an extremely extrovert life among the student community. After qualification he obtained resident appointments at St Thomas's, first as a casualty officer for six months and then for six months as house surgeon to Sir Charles Max Page and to "Joey" (R H O B) Robinson. On consulting the latter as to his future he was advised to get out of the rut of London and to carve out a name and a career in an area crying out for first-class original skill. As a result Colchester was to benefit and to become a recognised surgical centre. When he first went to Colchester in 1930 he had to start as a general-practitioner-surgeon but within two years he became solely a consultant, the first in what had always been a general-practitioner hospital; and before long he was coping with the surgery of a wide are of East Anglia. He spear-headed the development of the Essex County Hospital and was responsible for the creation of further consultant posts. His early years in general practice he always regarded as a valuable experience which enabled him to appreciate better the needs of the practitioners who called him in consultation. In addition to the Essex County Hospital, he did a great deal of valuable work on the surgery of tuberculosis at Black Notley Hospital, near Braintree, in association with M C Wilkinson. From the introduction of the National Health Service in 1948 he became a valuable member of the North East Metropolitan Regional Board on which he served until 1963, and he was a member of the Hospital Management Committee from 1948 to 1954. When the Research Committee of the Regional Board was inaugurated in 1956 Reid became its chairman, continuing until his premature death. He founded a surgical association for the region. He was a member of the editorial board of the British journal of surgery and introduced monthly Saturday clinical meetings of the Colchester Surgical Club, which attracted surgeons from all over the world, and he also found time to travel extensively, making surgical contacts in Europe and the United States of America.

A stocky, fair-haired, robust Scot usually with a twinkle in his eye, he was able to accomplish a vast amount of work. As a surgeon he was supremely competent, ingenious and in the van of progress, as instance his early mastery of the problems of fluid balance and of transurethral prostatectomy. As a man he was a true friend, without jealousy or malice, possessed of great powers of persuasion and administration, and ever ready to help his younger colleagues.

In his leisure he was a golfer and enjoyed fishing in his ancestral Scotland. He was also a talented artist and enjoyed the good things of a cultivated life to the full.

Latterly his health began to fail as he was emphysematous and liable to attacks of pulmonary infection. His passing left a gap difficult to fill. He married twice. By his first marriage, which was dissolved in 1960, he had four daughters and a son; one of his daughters, Alison Mary Deirdre, married Lord Primrose, heir of the Earl of Rosebery, in 1955. In 1961 he married Mrs Olive Gates of Boxford, who survived him. He died on 14 June 1968 in the Essex County Hospital, aged 62. He had lived for some years at Stoke-by-Nayland, but latterly at Dedham.

It has been difficult to trace the origins of the Reid's further back than Margie's grandparents, George and Helen Reid, who lived in Salisbury. The Reid family originated in Dumfries and Galloway, around the town of Moniaive. There are presumably distant relations still living there because Ronnie's family spent time there during World War II as a place of respite from Colchester.

Ronnie's mother was Helen Lorimer, from a well-known Dumfriesshire family, and her mother or grandmother was a Kirkpatrick.

Margie used to say that her aunt Peggy told her that their parents' origins were shrouded in mystery and that there was thought to be a secret love child who was somehow smuggled into the family through the Kirkpatrick connection. The Empress Eugenie of France or her sister Paca, Duchess of Alba were mentioned, both of whom were educated in England. There seems to be no evidence of this, however.

Ronnie Reid was a truly kind and charming man. I recall him giving me dinner at his club (the Savile) and wanting to put me up for membership (I declined with gratitude, citing the Groucho Marx response).

He was also a hugely popular local figure, having brought Colchester General Hospital to the forefront of medical excellence in the post World War II years. An exceptionally modest man, he liked to tell the story of the time when his car had broken down, and he found himself lost in deepest rural Essex, waiting for a bus. He got chatting with a local woman who, when she heard his name, told him that he was "very well thought of, in Thorpe-le-Soken". He felt at that moment, he said, a true local hero.

Ancestry Notes 5 – The Leemings

My maternal grandmother, Dorothy Caroline Leeming, was born in London in 1878 and married my grandfather Bertrand Russell in 1902.

The Leemings are an ancient Yorkshire and Lancashire Catholic recusant family. John Leeming (born1680) is recorded as living at Wolfen Hall, Chipping, Lancashire which he leased from Lord Derby in 1700. In 1715 he fought for the Jacobite cause and was subsequently outlawed, though allowed to return home three years later.

His grandson Thomas Leeming, born in 1760, was the first to enter commercial life, building and operating cotton mills in Preston and Manchester. The successful business was carried on by Thomas's two sons, John and Miles, under the business name of John Leeming & Co.

John Leeming, the elder son, moved to Adelphi House, Salford (now part of Salford University Media Centre), Manchester where he was a JP and Mayor, dying in 1847. After his death, his widow Elizabeth (nee Harrison) moved South with her unmarried children and is recorded in the 1861 census as living at Spring Grove, Richmond with her two sons John George (aged 41 – no occupation given) and Charles (aged 33- Barrister).

Elizabeth died in Richmond in 1870. Spring Grove was a substantial property with land to the West of Queen's Road, Richmond, now built over. Spring Grove Road marks the spot today. Spring Grove was then as it is now, a highly respectable place to live (being just round the corner from Margie's house in Pyrland Road, Richmond!).

Thomas Leeming, 1800

John George Leeming married late in life to Caroline Galassi Cumming, in 1871. She was the daughter born in 1838, of Caroline Galassi and William Cumming. She had five siblings. Her mother was from an Italian family who had settled in Soho in the previous century. William Cumming was a veteran of the Napoleonic wars and had served in the Commissariat of Wellington's army throughout the Peninsula campaign as a Deputy Commissary-General. His General Service Medal (awarded to veterans of that period) shows that he was present at the great battles of Barrosa, Salamanca, Vittoria and Toulouse. A remarkable achievement. He died in 1853 aged 73.

John George Leeming was 51 at the time of his marriage and his wife Caroline was aged 33. Although he was something of a gentleman of leisure, he must have been of substantial means (presumably inherited), as they moved to 77 Addison Road, Kensington where the 1881 census has them living there with their three children and three servants.

77 Addison Road, Kensington W8

John George and Caroline had three children: Mary (b.1874), Edward (b.1876) and Dorothy (b.1878). Their early years must have been pleasant but sadly did not last, because John George died in 1883 and Caroline in 1891. Thus Dorothy, the youngest, was just 13 years old at the time of her mother's death.

An orphan at a young age along with her siblings, Dorothy must have had a difficult time. Yet her father's estate at the time of his death in 1883 was valued at £126,175, a great deal of money in those days. This must have ensured that the children were well looked after. In 1891 she was living at Addison Road with six servants and a French governess at the time of her mother's death and is later recorded as living with her sister Mary, with her Aunt Charlotte also present, at Thornwood Lodge, Campden Hill, Kensington.

It was at this address at Campden Hill in June 1900, that a fundraising event in aid of victims of the Siege of Mafeking (a famous moment of the South African Boer War) was held, as advertised in The Times: By kind permission of the Misses Leeming – At Thornwood Lodge – A Musical Matinee and Garden Party in aid of the sufferers of Mafeking...Tickets One Guinea and Half a Guinea..

It had been in May of that year that Mafeking had been relieved after a 7-month siege by the Boers, by a British 'flying column' which included a detachment of the Royal Horse Artillery (Bertie's Regiment). Could this elegant fundraiser have perhaps been where romance started between Bertie and Dolly?

When Dorothy came to marry Bertrand Russell in 1902, she was 24 years old and probably a wealthy young lady – quite a catch in other words.

I have been unable to trace any but basic records for Dorothy's two siblings: her sister, Mary who died in 1950, married Harvey Staunton a businessman from the South of England and they lived at Sidmouth, on the South coast.

Her brother Edward, the last male Leeming survivor and thus the last hope for carrying forward the Leeming name, tragically died in 1899 aged just 22, not having married. It is recorded however, that he died following an epileptic fit, at Tadworth Court, Epsom – the country home of Sir Charles Russell, Bertie's father. At that particular time, Bertie was away serving in South Africa with his regiment. However, as my cousin Duncan puts it, in his research on the family:

"Somehow, out of this mess, a romance blossomed, which was to lead to the wedding at the Brompton Oratory in 1902. I suspect that young Edward Leeming had been a close friend of Bertie, possibly a school friend, and the Leemings and the Russells were on easy visiting terms."

Dorothy Caroline Leeming, 1890

Dorothy and Bertrand appear to have enjoyed a very happy married life although World War I meant that Bertrand would have been away on active service for most of that period. He served with distinction, winning a DSO in France and being twice wounded, so it must have been a worrying time.

Before the start of that terrible war, Dorothy bore four girls: Prudence, Ursula, Joan and Clodagh, who would all go on to blossom and marry in special ways. They all four were a huge influence on my life. It must have been the sensitive and loving upbringing that they received from Dorothy and Bertrand that turned them all into such intelligent, caring and wholly admirable people.

Bertrand retired at the end of the war with the rank of Lt Colonel and the couple probably looked forward to a long and happy retirement. Sadly, this was not to be. In 1920 Dorothy was diagnosed with MS (Multiple Sclerosis) and died the following year.

The family must have moved to London when Dorothy became ill, because the Probate records on her death, records the address then as 73 Pont Street, London SW1.

Finally, to return to Dolly's father John George Leeming, who died in 1883. There is a certain mystery around this man, about whom we know very little. My late cousin Duncan Brand, who did a lot of has this to say about John George:

"We discover from ancient genealogy, that John George Leeming has been awarded a Papal Knighthood, made a Knight of St Gregory, by Pope Pius IX. All this adds an air of mystery to John George. To all outward appearance he was a man who inherited significant wealth, and never did anything with it, who married too late in life to see his children grow up... and then attracted this approbation at the end. He must have had depths and achieved things that are hidden from us. We have no record of his early life, until he turns up aged 41, at his mother's house in Richmond".

It therefore seems likely that John George performed some significant act that greatly benefited the Catholic Church. According to the Catholic Herald: The Order of St Gregory is for conspicuous lay service to the Church on the recommendation of a diocesan bishop with the support of the papal nuncio. Whether this involved some great act of practical assistance or simply the payment of a large donation to the Church, we do not know.

It seems unlikely that we shall ever find an answer - unless someone asks the Pope.

Ancestry Notes 6 – Tylers

It has been difficult to trace any background family for Aileen Tyler, mother of my father, Stanford. She was the second wife of Harry Hunter Bunn. It seems that there was a family timber business in Cape Town, that was built up into a successful concern by Aileen's brother Micky. Peter Bunn, Aileen's youngest son, writes in his memoirs of receiving a visit from Micky in Camberley 'complete with third wife and Rolls Royce'. Peter goes on to say 'I recall how furious he was at the dock strike holding up his shipments of timber to Cape Town. He cancelled his order with British firms and turned his attention to Scandinavian woods, which he said greatly improved his business profits'. Micky sounds like quite a go-getter.

Aileen Tyler may have been born in South Africa or alternatively in East Anglia, where she seems to have stayed at times during the 1930's and 1940's. There is no apparent record of her birth. The name Tyler is English, originating from the French word 'Tuilier' which means what it says - a person who makes or puts tiles on roofs.

According to the certificate of her marriage to Harry Hunter Bunn, in Cape Town in 1903, Aileen was living at 9, Hope Street, Cape Town. Two witnesses who signed the certificate are CWB Tyler and JC Tyler, presumably relations. I have not been able to trace these at all. The certificate was kindly sent to me by Karen Barnard my distant cousin in South Africa, who is married to Mike Barnard, great grandson of Harry Hunter Bunn and his first wife Sarah.

The Tyler name is well known in South East England. Aileen is said to have claimed kinship to the famous Wat Tyler, leader of the 1381 Peasants Revolt, who was born in Kent.

History has it that Wat Tyler was supposedly a good man who was driven, with his fellow peasants, to desperate measures by the imposition of crippling taxes. History relates that he was slain by the King's officers as he met with the teenage King Richard II at Smithfield, at the gates of London. It was believed wrongly, that he had somehow threatened the King. Though Richard is usually depicted as a hero in this story, the facts are uncertain. I personally think that Wat Tyler was very badly treated.

Death of Wat Tyler in 1381 (British Library)

My cousin Vanessa Bunn (a grandchild of Aileen Tyler Bunn, like me) tells the story that one of her uncles (presumably the pro-active Uncle Micky mentioned above), wrote to the British Prime Minister in the 1960's demanding compensation for the unlawful killing of his ancestor Wat Tyler. Not surprisingly, he did not get very far.

Aileen is reported to have been a fine pianist and an imaginative cook, both probably useful attributes when you have a family of small children to keep happy.

Aileen's husband Harry died in 1926 and she lived on for a further 41 years.

An interesting insight is given by Isabel Annie Dunstan (daughter of Harry Hunter Bunn and his first wife Sarah), writing in her memoirs some years ago about the effect of her mother's death and her father's second marriage on her family:

"It was difficult managing without a mother, so father thought it best to take us to England, to an aunt and uncle, to be educated there as schools are not as they are today. It was an eye-opener to us all – the voyage there and back. Unfortunately, our education (at school in England) was cut short by my father marrying a young wife, so could not keep two homes going. To me it was a wonderful three years. I saw a number of places and learned to depend on myself. I am sorry to say our stepmother was not too kind and good to some of us. The old saying 'a stepmother makes a stepfather' in this case was true. I was married in 1902, just a year after my return from England. It was a big mistake as I was very young to take on such a big responsibility".

I have my cousin Karen Barnard to thank for this. Her comment on the memoir is as follows:

"The story is that to remove her from his and Aileen's responsibility, HHB married her at 19 to 39 year old Egbert Garcia, in 1905. They had two sons before he died in 1913. She then took over the raising of Lionel (her youngest brother). But as you can see, her memory of that time is a little inaccurate".

During her last years, Aileen seems to have struggled financially and physically. It seems that her husband had made some bad investment decisions, including an unproductive coal mine, which severely affected his estate on death.

As for Wat Tyler, it is virtually impossible to trace a blood line back to the fourteenth century, albeit that the Tyler family were convinced of their link. He remains another question mark in the Burn ancestry.

Ancestry Notes 7 - Chaytors

Margie's mother Elinor Mary Stuart Reid was born Elinor Mary Stuart. Her mother, Elinor Mary Chaytor, had married Percy Watt Stuart, whose family originated in Garstang, Lancashire and may have had connections back to Bonnie Prince Charlie (see above – The Stuarts).

The Chaytors are a very English family. They were prominent in the reign of Queen Elizabeth the First, in the sixteenth century and in 1546 Christopher Chaytor, then head of the family, married Elizabeth Clervaux, daughter of a more ancient family, who had come over with William the Conqueror in 1066. This gave the Chaytors great standing and lands including Croft, the family seat in North Yorkshire.

The following is an extract from the internet:

Croft is situated on the south bank of the river Tees, and, though lacking in the bolder and grander features of nature, there is a charming combination of hill and dale, with meadow, woodland, and stream. It comprises the townships of Croft, Dalton, and Stapleton, containing about 7,000 acres and 815 inhabitants. The area of the township of Croft is about 4,500 acres.

Croft was formerly the manor and residence of the ancient and knightly family of Clervaux, the first of whom accompanied the Conqueror to England, fought at the Battle of Hastings, and was rewarded with lands at Bootham, in Yorkshire. Soon afterwards they settled at Croft, and for more than three centuries their honoured name was associated with the place. They formed alliances with the noblest families of the district, and Sir Richard Clervaux, "the magnus of his house," who lies buried in the south aisle of Croft Church, claimed kinship with Edward IV and Richard III, as set forth in the inscription on his tomb. Another

Richard Clervaux, in the time of Henry VIII, dying without issue, his sister Elizabeth became his sole heir and representative of the family. She married Christopher Chaytor, Esq., of Butterby, Durham, who was surveyor-general of the counties of Durham and Northumberland, in the reign of Elizabeth. Her grandson, Sir William Chaytor, of Croft, was knighted by James I., during that monarch's progress from Edinburgh to London, to take possession of the English Crown. His second son Henry was a colonel in the royal army under Prince Rupert. He was governor of Bolton Castle, in Wensleydale, during the Parliamentary Wars, which place he valiantly defended until reduced to eat horse flesh, and then capitulated on honourable terms. His elder brother, Thomas Chaytor, Esq., succeeded his father, Sir William, in the possession of Croft, but after one descent his line terminated, and the estate was inherited by William Chaytor, of Butterby, whose grandfather, Thomas Chaytor, was the fourth son of Elizabeth, the Clervaux heiress, and had succeeded to the Butterby estate. This William was created a baronet in 1671. He married Peregrina a daughter of Sir Joseph Cradock, of Cradock Hall, Richmond, but his children pre-deceased him without issue, and he was succeeded in 1720 by his nephew, Henry Chaytor. The latter married Jane, daughter and, eventually, heiress of Matthew Smales, Esq., of Gilling.

Their son William, his successor, was created a baronet in 1831. This Sir William married Isabella, younger daughter, and co-heiress with her sister Anne, wife of his brother, John Clervaux, of John Carter, Esq., of Tunstall and Richmond. They had four sons and three daughters. Croft Hall ,the family's former residence, was vacated when Clervaux Castle, a castellated mansion with five towers, surrounded by an extensive park, was erected by Sir William Chaytor. However, the castle has since been demolished.

Christopher Chaytor, who married the Clervaux heiress in 1546, was a junior son, though eventual heir of one John Chaytor who is described as 'Merchant Adventurer of Newcastle'. He must have gained enough wealth and respectability to have Christopher brought up in the household of a Duke of Somerset and buy him the manor of Butterby .

The Clervaux were truly ancient. Said to have been Counts of Clervaux, an offshoot of the Dukes of Burgundy, the line is traceable straight back to Charlemagne (d. AD 814).

Sir William Chaytor, created first Baronet in 1831, must have been an astute businessman. He developed Witton Park Colliery, had banking interests and was a board member of the Stockton and Darlington Railway, Britain's first commercial line, which served the Colliery amongst other functions.

John Chaytor, son of Sir William and Isabella, decided to emigrate to the relatively newly-discovered, exciting country of New Zealand, and his younger brother Edward was happy to go with him. They set sail from England in the brig Thames City and landed in Wellington in November 1860. They went with the intention of farming, settling at Marlborough, near Picton in the North of the South Island.

Arthur, a third Chaytor brother, later joined John and Edward. Like his brothers he soon grew to love the land. Over the next few years the brothers developed their farming business and slowly added more and more to it.

John married Emma Fearon, daughter of a well-known retired ship's captain, Edward Fearon, who had taken up a property in the Awatere district, known as Marathon, a successful farming enterprise. Later still, a fourth brother Charles, joined them from England.

John Chaytor with his Stuart granddaughters, 1900

John purchased a property in Picton and then bought Marshlands. Marshlands stands today, still owned by the descendants of John Clervaux Chaytor and the brothers who also settled in the country and left their mark as pioneers.

There were thus, at the beginning of the twentieth century, thriving Chaytor dynasties on both England and New Zealand.

John Chaytor, Margie's great grandfather, seems to have been a remarkable person, an astute businessman with sound financial ideas, a man ahead of his times. The Chaytor brothers wrote letters back from New Zealand to the family in Yorkshire. Tony Lugg, to whom I am indebted for most of the information in this chapter, has been researching these letters:

'The letters give a very interesting picture. I thought John Chaytor followed three cousins of his out as a pioneer farmer. In fact the Chaytors like many north of England landowners found iron ore and coal on their estates which fuelled the industrial revolution and resulted in a big rush of cash into the bank account. Unlike many others in that situation they didn't splash the cash on high living and too much architecture but invested some of it in the Colonies. So John and his brothers were effectively sent out to open a branch office in NZ; while they started off learning the ropes at their cousins' sheep station Flaxbourne, John soon bought a large stretch of land nearby. That proved a disaster and was sold, after which John bought Marshlands. There he built up a substantial farming operation, was instrumental in setting up the NZ dairy industry and so on. But what I found so remarkable about him are the financial structures he put in place. Marshlands was established as a company from the outset, Chaytor & Co, and later encompassed all the other assets, the estates in Yorkshire that somehow devolved on him, coal mines in the Midlands, and so on. Not only that, all his children had equal shares in the company, girls as well as boys. Such financial planning was normally unheard of in the 1890s, and is pretty rare nowadays, I would have thought. Chaytor & co only split up after the war.'

Today there are flourishing branches of the Chaytors in both Yorkshire and New Zealand.

Ancestry Notes 8 – Lorimers

The Lorimers: Margie's paternal grandmother was Helen Lorimer. They are a highly respected Lowland Scots family, linked through marriage to other notable families such as the Moores of Glasgow and Eugenie, Empress of France.

The Lorimers became linked to the Moores when George Lorimer married Janet Moore in about 1785. George had been born at Ayr and later joined the army, serving in the American War of Independence as a purser with his friend Sir John Laurie of Maxwellton. Annnie Laurie of the eponymous song, was a cousin. George later became a schoolmaster at Glencairn, Dumfrieshire. His wife, Janet Moore, was from a large and illustrious Lowland Scottish family. Among her brothers were General Sir John Moore, the hero of Corunna, Surgeon James Carrick Moore and Admiral of the Fleet Sir Graham Moore.

George and Janet had seven children including John, born in 1795 and said to be a 'pious man', who married Anne Crinzean, daughter to the Factor of the Maitland family estates. They in turn produced seven children.

Their sixth child was Robert Lorimer, born in 1832. Robert married Helen Crosbie, daughter of Jean Kirkpatrick and William Crosbie. The 1861 and 1881 census both have them living at Morton in Dumfrieshire and Robert is described as 'shoemaker'. Robert and Helen duly produced seven more children (seven seems to have been a popular number with the Lorimers). Five of these children never married but two daughters took the plunge – Jessie married George Ollington (grandfather of Robin) and Helen married George Reid, father of Ronnie.

As mentioned above, Helen Lorimer, mother of Ronnie Reid, was the granddaughter of Jean Kirkpatrick, who married William Crosbie in about 1820. This Jean Kirkpatrick was a relation of William Kirkpatrick who, in the eighteenth century, set up in business as a wine merchant in Malaga, Spain. He became American Consul and a social and business success. His daughter Maria married the Count de Montijo and their daughter Eugenie de Montijo later became Empress of France, while her elder sister Maria, known as Paca, married the Duke of Alba (whose ancestry went back to James ll of England). Great names in high places indeed, though their genes have little to do with ours

Ronnie Reid's great-grandmother, Jean Kirkpatrick was a cousin of these Spain-based Kirkpatricks.

New Generations – The Durns and Banks

Our family tree is alive and flourishing. It continues strongly and will continue to do so for centuries, I trust. So far, I have only mentioned the genes that culminate in the DNA of Alex, Johnnie and Annabel, but it does not stop there. Alex and Johnnie have married and produced children who will hopefully in time, produce a further generation. By marrying, Jo Banks and Cathy Durn have brought exciting new elements into the family, thus keeping it healthily growing.

We can already see how successful this input has been, simply by observing young Alfie, Ben, Olivia, Oscar and Sophie. I need say no more.

Jo and Cathy have kindly provided details on their respective families and forbears which are set out on the following pages. These bring us fully up to date, and how welcome they are.

The Durns

The Durns come from the West of England. Ronald Durn married Cathy's mother Linda Wood and they soon emigrated to South Africa, where Cathy was born and educated. Following the breakup of the marriage in about 1995, Linda and her children returned to the UK. Cathy met Johnnie Burn in about the year 2000 and they married in 2004.

Cathy's mother's family also came from the West of England. Notable among them was her uncle Frederick Evans who served in the RAF during World War II and died for his country in 1942 after being shot down over Germany. Here is the official account - clearly, he was a very brave man.

Name: EVANS Name: Frederick Charles Date of Birth: 25 years Deceased / Burial: August 28, 1942 Family information: son of William EJ Evans and Sarah M. Evans. Husband of Renee IC Evans, Cinderford, Gloucstershire. Nationality: England Part: 1. RAF Photo Reconnaissance Unit. Rank: Sgt. Function: pilot Registration number: 521 752 Grave Location: A / 1/26

Tomb Inscriptions, At the going down of the sun and in the morning we will remember Him. Details: Alphen, crash August 28, 1942 Location: in a forest under Alphen. Time: 13:00 Cause: shot down by German fighter.

Crew: Sgt. FC Evans, slain Aircraft type: Vickers Supermarine Spitfire Mk.1; Serial no .: AB 422. Purpose: Probably Evans was commissioned to take pictures of the airfield Gilze-Rijen. Publication: Article Tilburg Courier sept. 1989 (G.Kobes): 1989 (G.Kobes): August 28, 1942. It is very warm and clear weather. The wind is east. We follow the journal of the LBD: Multiple Do.17 and one unidentified aircraft in various directions and div. heights. 10.40 - 11.40 As for 13.40 Multiple Do.17 and one Me.109 as 13:50 Bosch Brand North East.

This fire was caused by the crash of an airplane in a forest north-west of the village of Alphen. The plane burned almost completely. The forest fire van Alphen was very fast on the spot so that a large forest fire could be avoided. The aircraft, a Vickers Supermarine Spitfire Mk.1, was assigned to the 1. Photographic Reconnaissance Unit, so it can be assumed that the pilot had been commissioned to take pictures of the Gilze Rijen. Airport area At age 25, the pilot, Frederick Charles Evans from the English Gloucestershire, was buried at "Vredehof", section A, row 1, grave number 26. "At the going down of the sun and in the morning, we will remember him"

So many aspects of our family have been affected by world War II.

Cathy's daughter, Sophie Burn, has prepared an interesting family tree charting the genetic makeup of by country of origin. Here it is

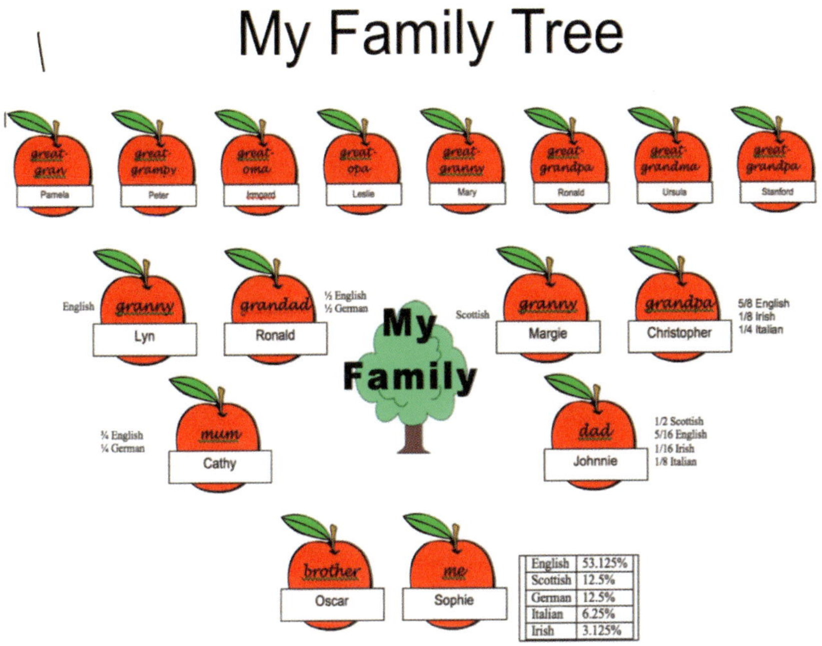

The Banks

The Banks family are Londoners. Jo's mother, Barbara Eileen Banks, was born in South London, in 1939. Her maiden name was Townsend.

Barbara says her father Edward Townsend left home as a boy to go to sea, because he fell out with his own father's new wife (his mother had died). He had a sister called Rose who died young and a younger brother Alfred, whom he would see sometimes. He did not like to talk about his family.

Barbara's mother had one brother, Frank and one sister, Joan. There was also another baby boy who sadly died in infancy. Born Eileen Fitzpatrick, she married Edward Townsend, who was in the Royal Navy, in 1937 and they had two daughters, Barbara and Anne. They lived in Balham, South London.

Barbara met Brian at a dance held over the ice rink in Streatham. She was 18 and working at the Bank of New Zealand and he was 19 and yet to start his successful career in the City. They married in 1962. Barbara says:

When I met Brian, he was working at the offices of a building company near Piccadilly. Then through a cricketing friend, he went to work for Moodies Services and got his first insight into the City.

From there, he went to stockbrokers Messels, as an investment Analyst. He wasn't comfortable working with colleagues there, who were mainly privileged public school types. But he soon grew confident and learnt that he was much better at his job than they were, and this was quickly recognised. He was there probably two years and at some time in that period, he sent a letter introducing himself to the high-profile City Investment Banker, Jim Slater, who was by then successfully operating his company - Slater Walker. This letter somehow got lost, but then a year later, was actually delivered. It had got wet at some point and some of his words were unreadable. Jim read his letter and was impressed. He replied to Brian, asking to meet him, and then asked Brian to join his company.

Everything went well for several years, until Slater fell out of favour in the City. He was labelled an 'Asset Stripper', which was very big news at the time. The company floundered and several of his staff were accused of being in league with him. Brian, with a few others, were not involved in that side of it. Their part of the company carried on.

Brian was then asked to join Mark Weinberg's company Allied Dunbar, on the investment side. That didn't last long, as he really wanted to start his own private investment company. That went well, as most things that he had dealings with did, but he was ambitious and always looking for better ways of working. He sold out, and started Guildhall Investment Management and later, Savoy Asset Management.

He was very popular and knew so many people. We were presented one year at the Mansion House and Brian was made a Freeman of the City of London. Maggie Thatcher was there also at the dinner that evening.'

My sister Jancis's eldest son, Sam Houston was starting a career as an Investment Manager in the City at this time and knew Brian Banks. He wrote to me:

I met up with Brian and his colleagues as well as my own team, in various haunts around Southwark, from time to time. The Balls Bros at the Corn Exchange and the Boot and Flogger spring particularly to mind!

The main point about him from my perspective was his friendly tolerance of a very junior acquaintance! In my experience he really was a very nice bloke with a great sense of fun, despite his slightly cut-throat reputation from the Slater Walker days (where the very idea of hostile takeovers was first hatched, I believe.) The world was a much simpler place in the late 1980s!

I will quickly add that his memorial service filled Southwark Cathedral, which is a good indication of his very many friends.

Indeed, his memorial service must have been quite an occasion. Here is an extract from a eulogy given on that occasion:

"Brian must have known a thousand people but he always made me feel I was one of his special mates. I expect nine hundred and ninety-nine others felt the same. He admired Barbara for the way she kept the family, particularly himself, in order and referred to her as 'Mother Earth'. He was proud of his children and constantly talked of what Andrew, Jo and Alex were up to, and he delighted in his grandchildren."

His greatest passion was sport – football, golf and especially, cricket. Brian played amateur league football for Sidcup Rangers, played in the first-ever floodlit game and was proud of scoring goals at all levels, including the FA Cup Competition.:

A day at Lords with good company and a hamper of food and wine was the pinnacle.

"My favourite days with Brian were spent at Lords. Efficient and urbane, Brian waiting behind the turnstiles: "late as usual, Green." Meeting friends and family, Brian's acute criticism of field placings and bowling changes through the morning. The essential meeting with others in the Bar behind the Pavilion. The twenty minutes taken to cover the thirty yards, while Brian was greeted by Stewards, Groundsmen, Test Players, Committee Members and retired Umpires:

"Hello, Brian"
"Dennis, old boy!"

"Brian"
"Hello Alec".
Arrival at the Bar:
"Hey, Banksie – What'll it be?"
"Champagne of course, old boy."
And at the end of the day's proceedings, the arrival of his faithful, regular cabbie:
"Take me home, but see if we can find a little hostelry before we drop Mr Green off."

His sudden and untimely death in 1999, at the early age of 61, was a shock to his family, friends and colleagues. Announcing this, his company Savoy Asset Management said:

Brian Banks, director of Savoy Asset Management, has died at the age of 61. A former investment manager at Slater Walker, he was renowned as a champion stock picker. He looked after a fanatically loyal list of clients at Savoy subsidiary, Guildhall.

Banks' insights, decency and lively approach to life are sorely missed by the many practitioners across the City of London with whom he did business.

Barbara's sister Anne married John Keenan in 1964, and they lived near Barbara and Brian in South London, having three children – Jane, Matthew and Vicky. John sadly died in 2015.

The Grandchildren today are all I could possibly wish:

Sophie, Ben, Alfie, Oscar, Olivia, 2020

DNA TESTS

Margie's DNA was tested in 2014, when Edinburgh University conducted tests to identify Royal Stuart DNA. Though I have not seen the results, I understand that Margie's DNA produced a close match with Royal Stuart DNA obtained from Charles Edward Stuart, The Young Pretender's Polish descendants, through Charlotte, Duchess of Albany (his illegitimate daughter, later recognised as his daughter, by his Scottish mistress Clementina Walkinshaw). The likelihood is that this DNA match comes via Margie's possible descent from Clementina Johannes Sobieski Douglass (The Young Pretender's purported other daughter known as the Finsthwaite Princess) as detailed in the Ancestry Notes on the Stuarts. This would appear to substantiate the proposition of a bloodline via her mother, Elinor Mary Reid (Stuart). As detailed in the Ancestry Notes on the Stuarts, this hinges on the story of a secret illegitimate daughter of Charles Edward and his Scottish mistress, Clementina Walkinshaw. This DNA match provides strong backing to the story.

Apart from this aspect, I believe that Margie's DNA was unremarkable as it contained mainly Scottish and English components, as one would expect.

My own DNA was tested in November 2020. Unsurprisingly, the results reveal a mainly Irish and English background (the Russell's being mainly Irish and the Burns mainly English in origin). There are elements (7.5%) of Southern European DNA (Italian, Greek and Balkan) presumably from my great grandmother, Caroline Galassi Cumming.

Strangely, there also appears 1.3% Mesoamerican and Andean genes. Quite where they came from is anyone's guess. Perhaps the Tylers (paternal grandmother) or the Leemings (maternal grandmother) could explain. Or perhaps, it's another way of saying 'Neanderthal'. I rather like this mystery – the secret je ne sais quoi element that turns a humdrum dish into a culinary delight.

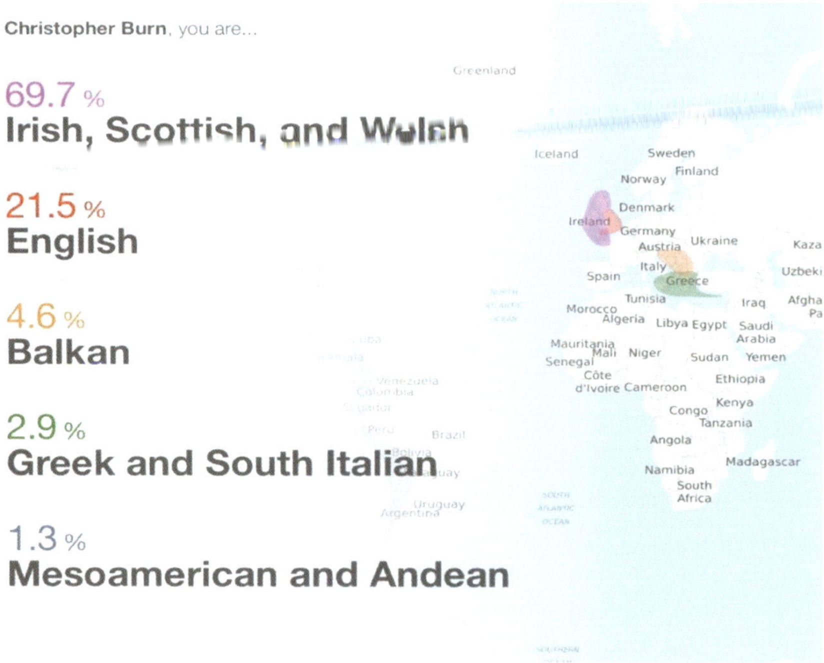

Result of DNA test on C Burn by MyHeritage, November 2020.

FAMILY TREES

SUMMARY OF THE BURN FAMILY TREES

from NW England	*from NW England*	*From Kent related to Wat Tyler Peasants Revolt 1381*	*No details*	*Lord Chief Justice of England - Anglo Irish Norman roots*	*Belfast Doctor's family*	*Londoner - from Lancashire originally*	*Italian - husband William Cumming - Londoner*	*No details*	*No details*	*Lowland Scottish family*	*Lowland Scottish family*	*From Lake District - link to Bonnie Prince Charlie*	*London County Council member*	*Landowner in Yorkshire and NZ farm estates*	*NZ farm estates*
Henry Bunn 1812-1864 ↘	Isabella Hunter 1821-1876 ↓	No details ↓	No details ↙	Sir Charles Russell 1832-1900 ↘	Ellen Mulholland 1858-1900 ↓	John Leeming 1820-1883 ↓	Caroline Galassi Cumming 1838-1891 ↙	No details ↘	No details ↓	Robert Lorimer 1832-1916 ↓	Helen Crosbie 1842-1907 ↙	William B Stuart [illegible]35-1904 ↘	Elizabeth Straker 1839-1911 ↓	John Chaytor 1836-1920 ↓	Emma Fearon 1840-1913 ↙
	Harry H Bunn 1859-1926	Aileen Tyler 1882-1967 ↓			Bertrand Russell 1876-1968 ↓	Dorothy Leeming 1878-1922			George Reid 1874-1959	Helen Lorimer 1874-1956 ↓			Percy W Stuart 1869-1948 ↓	Elinor M Chaytor 1874-1917	
		Stanford Burn 1904-1941			Ursula Russell 1905-1942					Ronnie W Reid 1906-1968			Elinor M Stuart 1905-1978		
			↓									↓			
			Christpher Burn 1940-									Mar[illegible] Reid 1940-			
								↓				↓			
			Alex Burn 1968- ↓ m	Joanne Banks 1967-				Johnnie Burn 1970- ↓ m	Cathy Durn 1967-			Anna[illegible] Burn 1979-	Rob Katschmaryk		
		Alfie Burn 2002-	Ben Burn 2004-	Olivia Burn 2007-				Oscar Burn 2007-	Sophie Burn 2009-						

BURN FAMILY SUMMARY

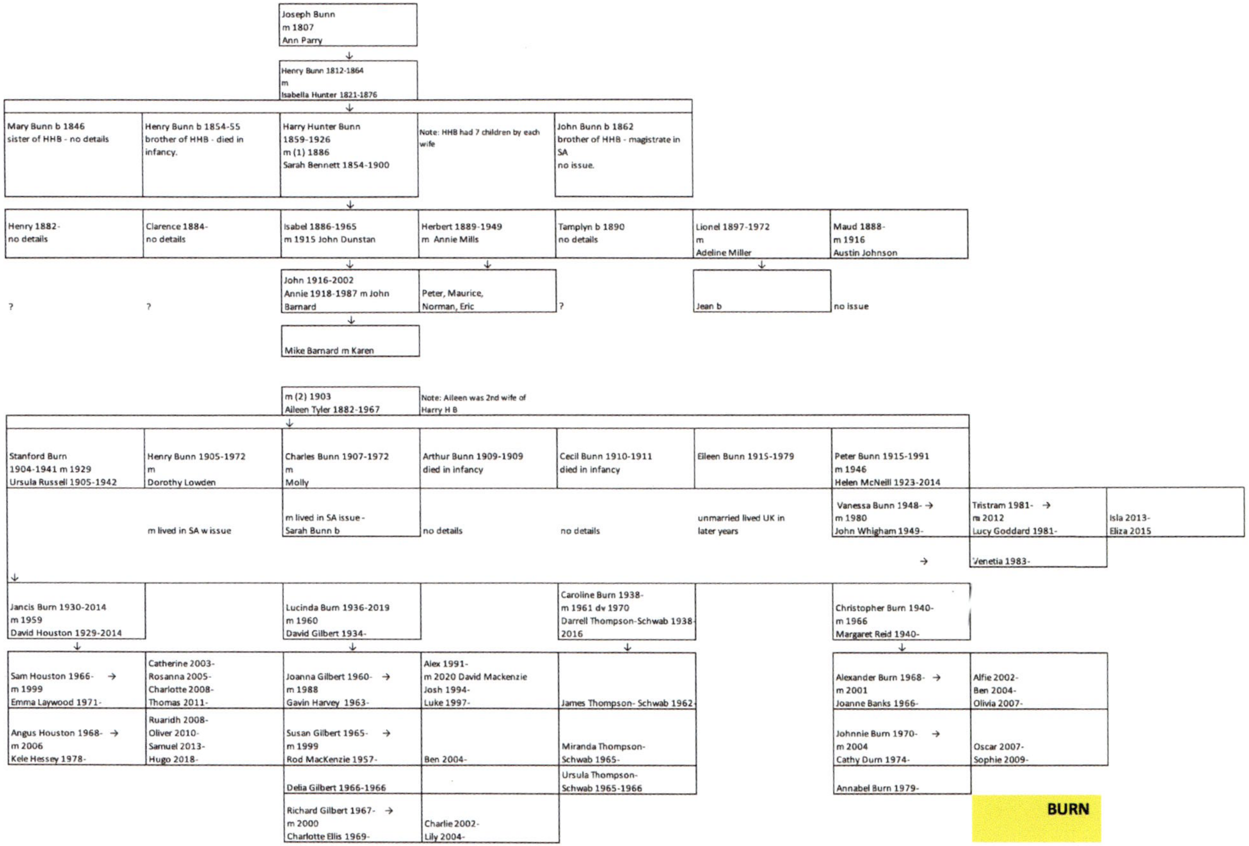
BURN
Joseph Bunn m 1807 Ann Parry
Henry Bunn 1812-1864 m Isabella Hunter 1821-1876
Mary Bunn b 1846 sister of HHB - no details
Henry Bunn b 1854-55 brother of HHB - died in infancy.
Harry Hunter Bunn 1859-1926 m (1) 1886 Sarah Bennett 1854-1900
Note: HHB had 7 children by each wife
John Bunn b 1862 brother of HHB - magistrate in SA no issue.
Henry 1882- no details
Clarence 1884- no details
Isabel 1886-1965 m 1915 John Dunstan
Herbert 1889-1949 m Annie Mills
Tamplyn b 1890 no details
Lionel 1897-1972 m Adeline Miller
Maud 1888- m 1916 Austin Johnson
?
?
John 1916-2002 Annie 1918-1987 m John Barnard
Peter, Maurice, Norman, Eric
?
Jean b
no issue
Mike Barnard m Karen
m (2) 1903 Aileen Tyler 1882-1967
Note: Aileen was 2nd wife of Harry H B
Stanford Burn 1904-1941 m 1929 Ursula Russell 1905-1942
Henry Bunn 1905-1972 m Dorothy Lowden
m lived in SA w issue
Charles Bunn 1907-1972 m Molly
m lived in SA issue - Sarah Bunn b
Arthur Bunn 1909-1909 died in infancy
no details
Cecil Bunn 1910-1911 died in infancy
no details
Eileen Bunn 1915-1979
unmarried lived UK in later years
Peter Bunn 1915-1991 m 1946 Helen McNeill 1923-2014
Vanessa Bunn 1948- m 1980 John Whigham 1949-
Tristram 1981- m 2012 Lucy Goddard 1981-
Isla 2013- Eliza 2015
Venetia 1983-
Jancis Burn 1930-2014 m 1959 David Houston 1929-2014
Lucinda Burn 1936-2019 m 1960 David Gilbert 1934-
Caroline Burn 1938- m 1961 dv 1970 Darrell Thompson-Schwab 1938-2016
Christopher Burn 1940- m 1966 Margaret Reid 1940-
Sam Houston 1966- m 1999 Emma Laywood 1971-
Catherine 2003- Rosanna 2005- Charlotte 2008- Thomas 2011-
Angus Houston 1968- m 2006 Kele Hessey 1978-
Ruaridh 2008- Oliver 2010- Samuel 2013- Hugo 2018-
Joanna Gilbert 1960- m 1988 Gavin Harvey 1963-
Alex 1991- m 2020 David Mackenzie Josh 1994- Luke 1997-
Susan Gilbert 1965- m 1999 Rod MacKenzie 1957-
Ben 2004-
Delia Gilbert 1966-1966
Richard Gilbert 1967- m 2000 Charlotte Ellis 1969-
Charlie 2002- Lily 2004-
James Thompson- Schwab 1962-
Miranda Thompson-Schwab 1965-
Ursula Thompson-Schwab 1965-1966
Alexander Burn 1968- m 2001 Joanne Banks 1966-
Alfie 2002- Ben 2004- Olivia 2007-
Johnnie Burn 1970- m 2004 Cathy Dum 1974-
Oscar 2007- Sophie 2009-
Annabel Burn 1979-

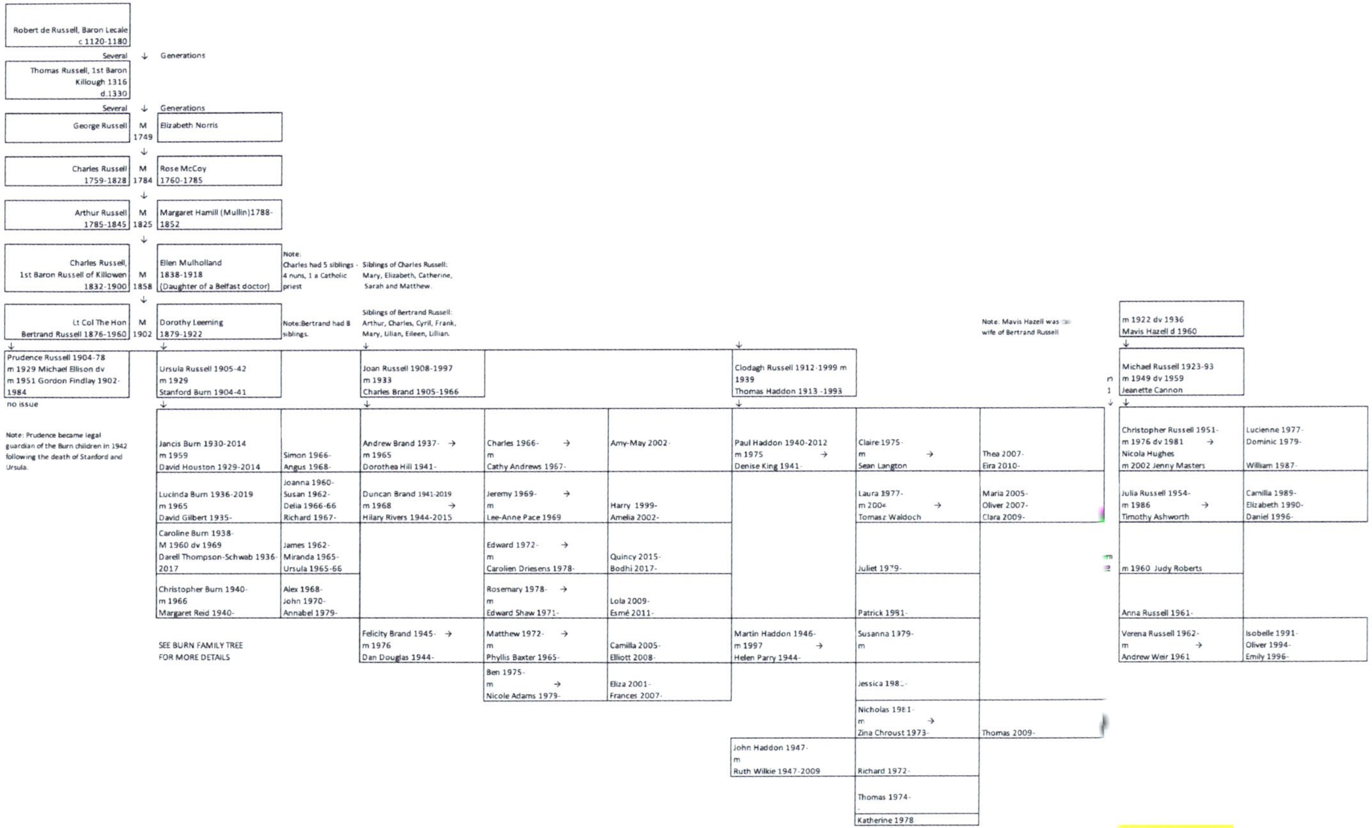
Robert de Russell, Baron Lecale c.1120-1180
Several Generations
Thomas Russell, 1st Baron Killough 1316 d.1330
Several Generations
George Russell M 1749 Elizabeth Norris
Charles Russell 1759-1828 M 1784 Rose McCoy 1760-1785
Arthur Russell 1785-1845 M 1825 Margaret Hamill (Mullin)1788-1852
Charles Russell, 1st Baron Russell of Killowen 1832-1900 M 1858 Ellen Mulholland 1838-1918 (Daughter of a Belfast doctor)
Note: Charles had 5 siblings - 4 nuns, 1 a Catholic priest
Siblings of Charles Russell: Mary, Elizabeth, Catherine, Sarah and Matthew.
Lt Col The Hon Bertrand Russell 1876-1960 M 1902 Dorothy Leeming 1879-1922
Note:Bertrand had 8 siblings.
Siblings of Bertrand Russell: Arthur, Charles, Cyril, Frank, Mary, Lilian, Eileen, Lillian.
Note: Mavis Hazell was wife of Bertrand Russell
m 1922 dv 1936 Mavis Hazell d 1960
Prudence Russell 1904-78 m 1929 Michael Ellison dv m 1951 Gordon Findlay 1902-1984
no issue
Note: Prudence became legal guardian of the Burn children in 1942 following the death of Stanford and Ursula.
Ursula Russell 1905-42 m 1929 Stanford Burn 1904-41
Joan Russell 1908-1997 m 1933 Charles Brand 1905-1966
Clodagh Russell 1912-1999 m 1939 Thomas Haddon 1913 -1993
Michael Russell 1923-93 m 1949 dv 1959 Jeanette Cannon
Jancis Burn 1930-2014 m 1959 David Houston 1929-2014
Simon 1966- Angus 1968-
Lucinda Burn 1936-2019 m 1965 David Gilbert 1935-
Joanna 1960- Susan 1962- Delia 1966-66 Richard 1967-
Caroline Burn 1938- M 1960 dv 1969 Darell Thompson-Schwab 1936-2017
James 1962- Miranda 1965- Ursula 1965-66
Christopher Burn 1940- m 1966 Margaret Reid 1940-
Alex 1968- John 1970- Annabel 1979-
SEE BURN FAMILY TREE FOR MORE DETAILS
Andrew Brand 1937- m 1965 Dorothea Hill 1941-
Charles 1966- m Cathy Andrews 1967-
Amy-May 2002-
Duncan Brand 1941-2019 m 1968 Hilary Rivers 1944-2015
Jeremy 1969- m Lee-Anne Pace 1969
Harry 1999- Amelia 2002-
Edward 1972- m Carolien Driesens 1978-
Quincy 2015- Bodhi 2017-
Rosemary 1978- m Edward Shaw 1971-
Lola 2009- Esmé 2011-
Felicity Brand 1945- m 1976 Dan Douglas 1944-
Matthew 1972- m Phyllis Baxter 1965-
Camilla 2005- Elliott 2008-
Ben 1975- m Nicole Adams 1979-
Eliza 2001- Frances 2007-
Paul Haddon 1940-2012 m 1975 Denise King 1941-
Claire 1975- m Sean Langton
Thea 2007- Eira 2010-
Laura 1977- m 2004 Tomasz Waldoch
Maria 2005- Oliver 2007- Clara 2009-
Juliet 1979-
Patrick 1981-
Martin Haddon 1946- m 1997 Helen Parry 1944-
Susanna 1979- m
Jessica 198_-
Nicholas 1981- m Zina Chroust 1973-
Thomas 2009-
John Haddon 1947- m Ruth Wilkie 1947-2009
Richard 1972-
Thomas 1974-
Katherine 1978
Christopher Russell 1951- m 1976 dv 1981 Nicola Hughes m 2002 Jenny Masters
Lucienne 1977- Dominic 1979-
William 1987-
Julia Russell 1954- m 1986 Timothy Ashworth
Camilla 1989- Elizabeth 1990- Daniel 1996-
m 1960 Judy Roberts
Anna Russell 1961-
Verena Russell 1962- m Andrew Weir 1961
Isobelle 1991- Oliver 1994- Emily 1996-

RUSSELL

Previous Generations
See notes

↓

Nicholas Backhouse
1782-1842
m 1806
Betty Stuart 1782-1879

↓

William Backhouse Stuart 1807-1866
m
Mary Anne Cremer Watt 1807-1879

Note: Believed to have married at Gretna around 1826 Both under age - MACW was daughter of Alexander Watt and Mary Barrett of Barbados

↓

Elizabeth Backhouse Stuart
1833-1861
m 1857
Albert Tomson

no issue

William W Backhouse Stuart
1835-1904
m 1862
Elizabeth Miriam Straker 1839-1911

↓

Elizabeth Stuart 1862-
(Opera singer, friend of Jenny Lind)

no issue

Herbert Stuart 1864-
m
Annie Taverner

↓

Gordon Stuart d 1917
m ?
Erica ?

no issue

Mabel Stuart 1866-1937

no issue

Percy Watt Stuart
1869-1948
m 1906
Elinor Mary Chaytor 1874-1917

↓

Elinor Mary Stuart
1905-1978
m 1929 Ronald Reid
1906-1968

↓

Deirdre Reid 1931-
m 1955 →
Neil Rosebery 1928-

Lucy 1955- Caroline 1964-
Jane 1960- Harry 1967-
Emma 1962-

Griselda Reid 1935-2001
m 1956 →
Peter Franks d 1978

Philip 1958-
Stephen 1959-
Elizabeth 1963-
William 1964-

Frances Reid 1940-1978
m 1964 →
Mike Eagar 1934-2019

Charlotte 1965-
Sophie 1967-

Margaret Reid 1940-
m 1966 →
Christopher Burn 1940-

Alexander 1968-
Johnnie 1970-
Annabel 1979-

David Reid 1946-
m 1971 →
Christine Reeves 1949-

James 1972-
Emily 1979-
Henrietta 1981-
Alice 1988-

SEE REID FAMILY TREE

Beatrice Stuart 1909-1994
m 1949
Hugh Sykes d 1950

no issue

Margaret Stuart 1913-2007
m 1937
Peter Lugg

↓

Anthony Lugg 1941-

Susan Lugg 1946-
m 19 dv 19 →
James Stevenson

Heloise Stevenson 1967-
m Robert Broughton 1968-2016 →
m 1993 Iain Henderson

Max 1997-
Charlie 1999-

James Stevenson 1973-

Rupert Stevenson 1976-

Mary Stuart d 1941
m
Frank Hankinson

↓

Robert Stuart 1900-1947
Margot (Shearing)
Hylda
Mollie

STUART

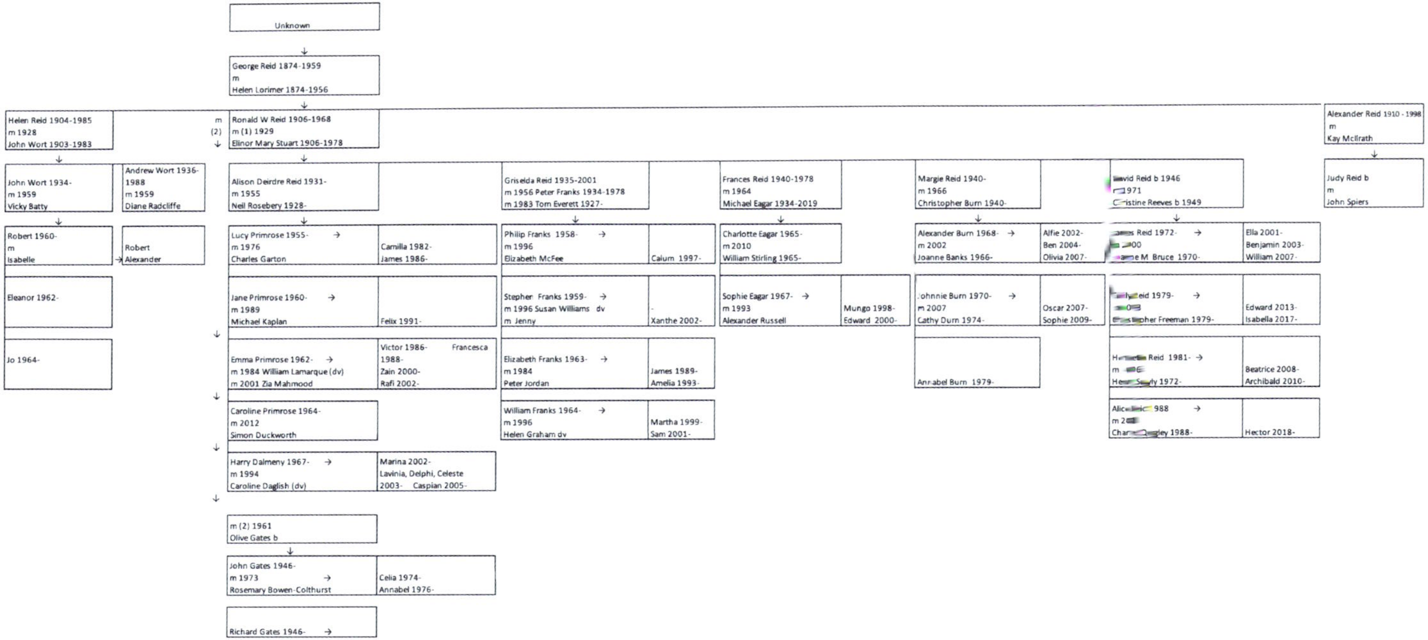

Unknown
George Reid 1874-1959
m
Helen Lorimer 1874-1956
Helen Reid 1904-1985
m 1928
John Wort 1903-1983
m
(2)
Ronald W Reid 1906-1968
m (1) 1929
Elinor Mary Stuart 1906-1978
Alexander Reid 1910 - 1998
m
Kay McIlrath
John Wort 1934-
m 1959
Vicky Batty
Andrew Wort 1936-
1988
m 1959
Diane Radcliffe
Robert 1960-
m
Isabelle
Robert
Alexander
Eleanor 1962-
Jo 1964-
Alison Deirdre Reid 1931-
m 1955
Neil Rosebery 1928-
Lucy Primrose 1955-
m 1976
Charles Garton
Camilla 1982-
James 1986-
Jane Primrose 1960-
m 1989
Michael Kaplan
Felix 1991-
Emma Primrose 1962-
m 1984 William Lamarque (dv)
m 2001 Zia Mahmood
Victor 1986-
Francesca
1988-
Zain 2000-
Rafi 2002-
Caroline Primrose 1964-
m 2012
Simon Duckworth
Harry Dalmeny 1967-
m 1994
Caroline Daglish (dv)
Marina 2002-
Lavinia, Delphi, Celeste
2003-
Caspian 2005-
m (2) 1961
Olive Gates b
John Gates 1946-
m 1973
Rosemary Bowen-Colthurst
Celia 1974-
Annabel 1976-
Richard Gates 1946-
Griselda Reid 1935-2001
m 1956 Peter Franks 1934-1978
m 1983 Tom Everett 1927-
Philip Franks 1958-
m 1996
Elizabeth McFee
Calum 1997-
Stephen Franks 1959-
m 1996 Susan Williams dv
m Jenny
Xanthe 2002-
Elizabeth Franks 1963-
m 1984
Peter Jordan
James 1989-
Amelia 1993-
William Franks 1964-
m 1996
Helen Graham dv
Martha 1999-
Sam 2001-
Frances Reid 1940-1978
m 1964
Michael Eagar 1934-2019
Charlotte Eagar 1965-
m 2010
William Stirling 1965-
Sophie Eagar 1967-
m 1993
Alexander Russell
Mungo 1998-
Edward 2000-
Margie Reid 1940-
m 1966
Christopher Burn 1940-
Alexander Burn 1968-
m 2002
Joanne Banks 1966-
Alfie 2002-
Ben 2004-
Olivia 2007-
Johnnie Burn 1970-
m 2007
Cathy Durn 1974-
Oscar 2007-
Sophie 2009-
Annabel Burn 1979-
vid Reid b 1946
1971
istine Reeves b 1949
s Reid 1972-
00
e M Bruce 1970-
Ella 2001-
Benjamin 2003-
William 2007-
eid 1979-
pher Freeman 1979-
Edward 2013-
Isabella 2017-
Reid 1981-
m
1972-
Beatrice 2008-
Archibald 2010-
988
m 2
ley 1988-
Hector 2018-
Judy Reid b
m
John Spiers

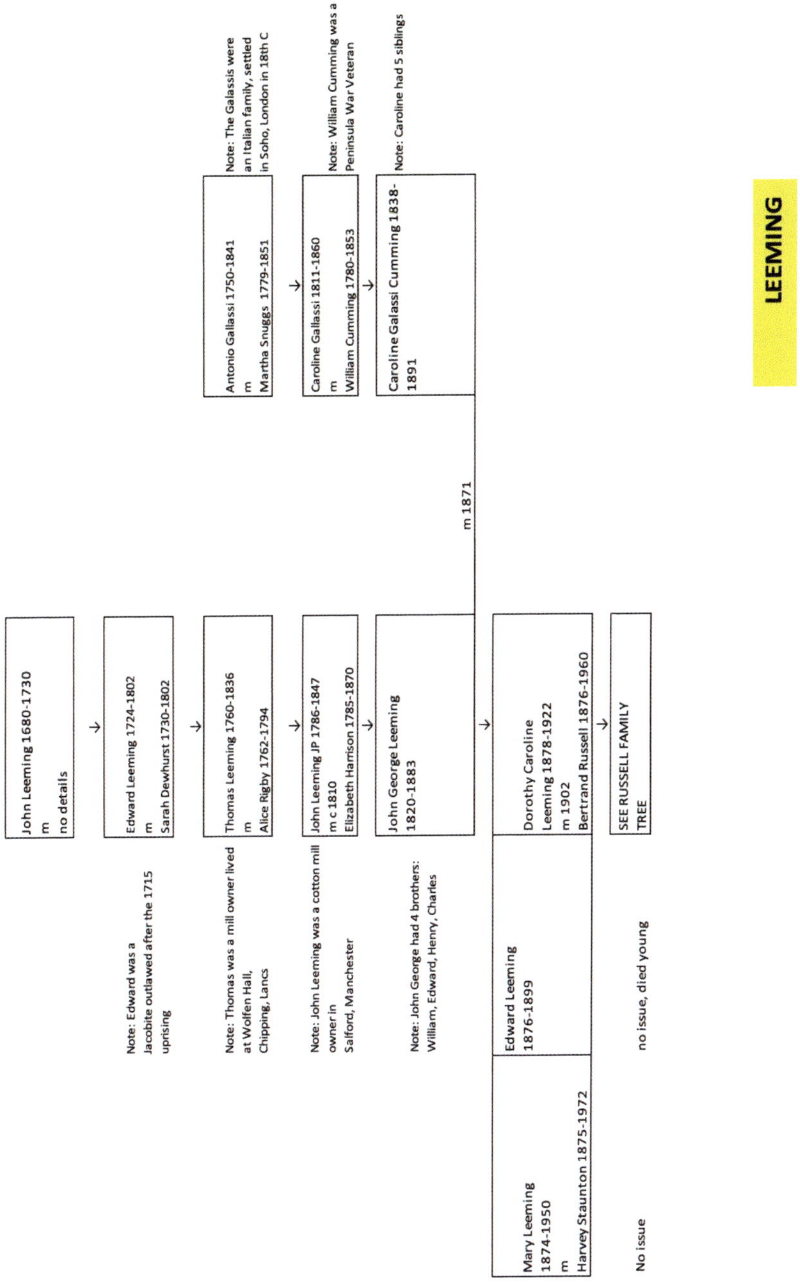
LEEMING
John Leeming 1680-1730 m no details
Edward Leeming 1724-1802 m Sarah Dewhurst 1730-1802
Note: Edward was a Jacobite outlawed after the 1715 uprising
Thomas Leeming 1760-1836 m Alice Rigby 1762-1794
Note: Thomas was a mill owner lived at Wolfen Hall, Chipping, Lancs
John Leeming JP 1786-1847 m c 1810 Elizabeth Harrison 1785-1870
Note: John Leeming was a cotton mill owner in Salford, Manchester
John George Leeming 1820-1883
Note: John George had 4 brothers: William, Edward, Henry, Charles
Antonio Gallassi 1750-1841 m Martha Snuggs 1779-1851
Note: The Galassis were an Italian family, settled in Soho, London in 18th C
Caroline Gallassi 1811-1860 m William Cumming 1780-1853
Note: William Cumming was a Peninsula War Veteran
Caroline Galassi Cumming 1838-1891
Note: Caroline had 5 siblings
m 1871
Mary Leeming 1874-1950 m Harvey Staunton 1875-1972
No issue
Edward Leeming 1876-1899
no issue, died young
Dorothy Caroline Leeming 1878-1922 m 1902 Bertrand Russell 1876-1960
SEE RUSSELL FAMILY TREE

Note: Harry H B m 1st wife Sarah Bennett - 7 children

Aileen Tyler
1882-1967
m 1903
Harry H Bunn
1859-1926

Note: Aileen was 2nd wife of Harry H B

Stanford Burn 1904-1941 m 1929 Ursula Russell 1905-1942	Henry Bunn 1905-1972 m Dorothy Lowden	Charles Bunn 1907-1972 m Molly	Arthur Bunn 1909-1909 died in infancy	Cecil Bunn 1910-1911 died in infancy	Eileen Bunn 1915-1979	Peter Bu[illegible]1915-1991 m 1946 Helen Mc[illegible]l
Note: S changed name from Bunn to Burn by Deed Poll in 1933 SEE BURN FAMILY TREE	m lived in SA w issue	Sarah Bunn 1945-	no details	no details	unmarried lived UK in later years	Vanessa Bu[illegible]1948- m 1980 John Whigh[illegible]1949-

Tristram Whi[illegible] m 1981- m 2012 Lucy Goddard [illegible]1-	Venetia Whigham 1983-
Isla 2013-	Eliza 2015-

TYLER

CHAYTOR

Christopher Chaytor
m 1596
Elizabeth Clervaux

↓

Several Generations

↓

Sir William Chaytor 1st Bt.
1771-1847
m 1803 Isabella Carter d 1855

↓

John Clervaux Chaytor 1806-1894
m 1834 Lydia Brown d 1889

Note: John Clervaux Chaytor had three siblings - he was the second eldest -

William 1805-1874
Matthew 1807-1882
Isabella 1810-1886

↓

John Clervaux Chaytor 1836-1920
m 1867 Emma Fearon d 1913

Arthur Chaytor 1843-1937
m 1872 Mary Burrell d 1898
m (2) 1903 Mary Allen d 1951

Note: Arthur had five children: Kathleen, Arthur, Frances, Frank, Walter

↓

Elinor Mary Chaytor 1874-1917 m 1906
Percy Watt Stuart

Note: Elinor Mary Chaytor had ten siblings - she was second eldest -

Beatrice, Isabel, Edward
Jane, Alfred, D'arcy,
Constance, Lawrence,
Frances, John

↓

Elinor Mary Stuart 1905-1978
m 1929
Ronald Reid 1906-1968

Beatrice Stuart 1909-1994
m 1949
Hugh Sykes d 1950

no issue

Margaret Stuart 1913-2007
m 1937
Peter Lugg

↓

Deirdre Reid b 1931
m 1955
Neil Rosebery
→ Lucy 1955- Caroline 1964-
Jane 1960- Harry 1967-
Emma 1962-

Griselda Reid 1935-2001
m 1956
Peter Franks d 1978
→ Philip 1958-
Stephen 1959-
Elizabeth 1963-
William 1964-

Frances Reid 1940-1978
m 1964
Mike Eagar 1934-2019
→ Charlotte 1965-
Sophie 1967-

Margaret Reid 1940-
m 1966
Christopher Burn 1940-
→ Alexander 1968-
Johnnie 1970-
Annabel 1979-

David Reid 1946-
m 1971
Christine Reeves 1949-
→ James 1972-
Emily 1979-
Henrietta 1981-
Alice 1988-

SEE REID FAMILY TREE

↓

Anthony Lugg 1941-

Susan Lugg 1946-
m 19 dv 19
James Stevenson
→ Heloise Stevenson 1967-
m Robert Broughton dv
m 1993 Iain Henderson
→ Max 1997-
Charlie 1999-

James Stevenson 1973-

Rupert Stevenson 1976-

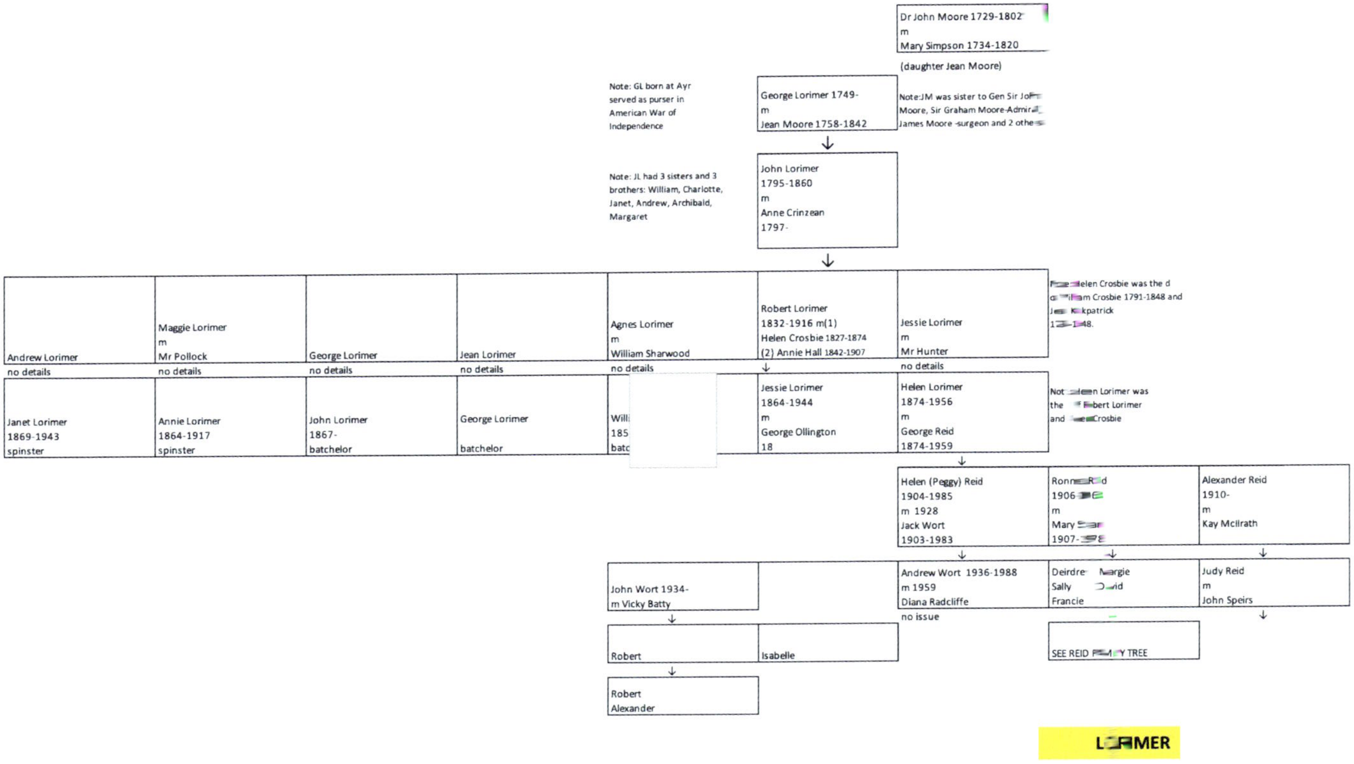
Dr John Moore 1729-1802
m
Mary Simpson 1734-1820
(daughter Jean Moore)
Note: GL born at Ayr served as purser in American War of Independence
George Lorimer 1749-
m
Jean Moore 1758-1842
Note:JM was sister to Gen Sir Jo
Moore, Sir Graham Moore-Admir
James Moore -surgeon and 2 othe
Note: JL had 3 sisters and 3 brothers: William, Charlotte, Janet, Andrew, Archibald, Margaret
John Lorimer
1795-1860
m
Anne Crinzean
1797-
Andrew Lorimer
no details
Maggie Lorimer
m
Mr Pollock
no details
George Lorimer
no details
Jean Lorimer
no details
Agnes Lorimer
m
William Sharwood
no details
Robert Lorimer
1832-1916 m(1)
Helen Crosbie 1827-1874
(2) Annie Hall 1842-1907
Jessie Lorimer
m
Mr Hunter
no details
elen Crosbie was the d
m Crosbie 1791-1848 and
kpatrick
48.
Janet Lorimer
1869-1943
spinster
Annie Lorimer
1864-1917
spinster
John Lorimer
1867-
batchelor
George Lorimer
batchelor
Will
185
batc
Jessie Lorimer
1864-1944
m
George Ollington
18
Helen Lorimer
1874-1956
m
George Reid
1874-1959
n Lorimer was
the bert Lorimer
and Crosbie
Helen (Peggy) Reid
1904-1985
m 1928
Jack Wort
1903-1983
1906
m
Mary
1907-
Alexander Reid
1910-
m
Kay Mcilrath
John Wort 1934-
m Vicky Batty
Andrew Wort 1936-1988
m 1959
Diana Radcliffe
no issue
Deirdre
Sally
Francie
Judy Reid
m
John Speirs
Robert
Isabelle
SEE REID TREE
Robert
Alexander
MER

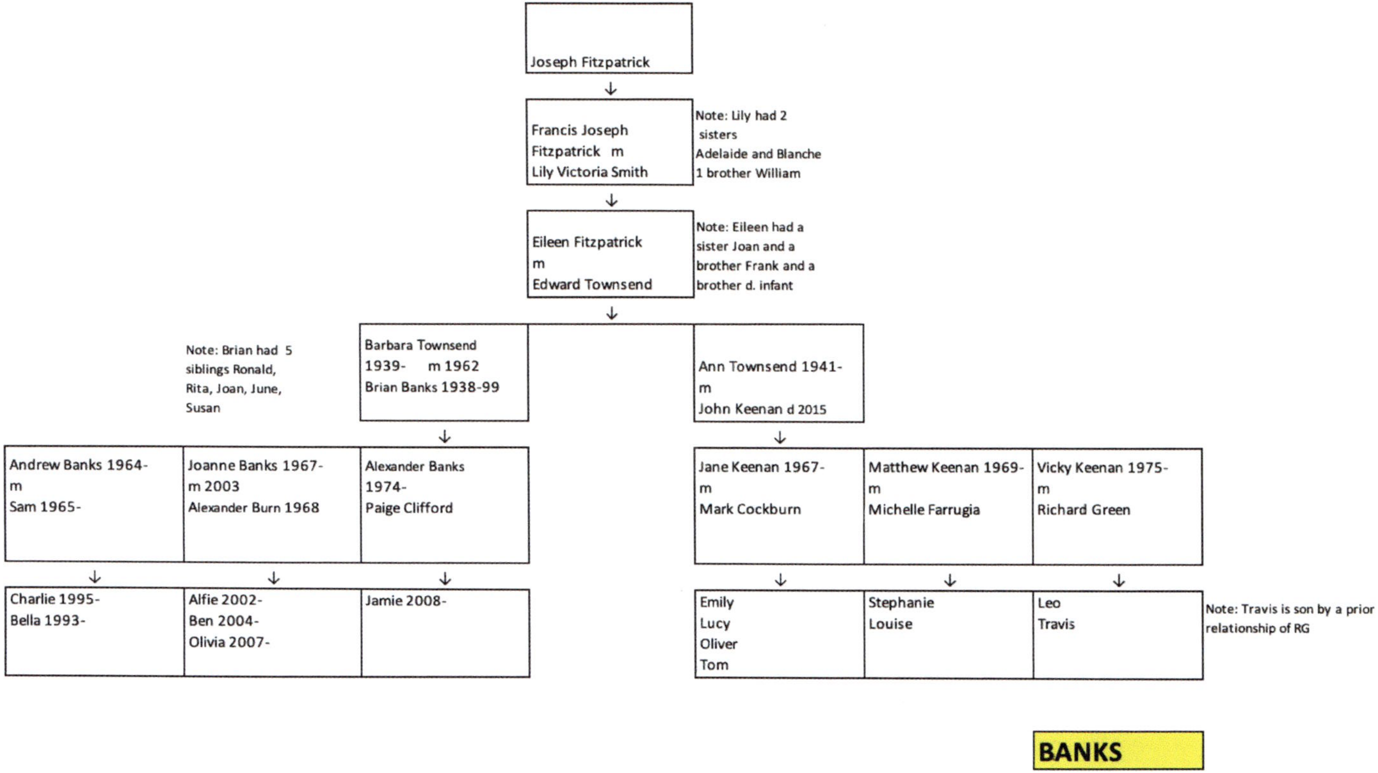
Joseph Fitzpatrick
Francis Joseph Fitzpatrick m Lily Victoria Smith
Note: Lily had 2 sisters Adelaide and Blanche 1 brother William
Eileen Fitzpatrick m Edward Townsend
Note: Eileen had a sister Joan and a brother Frank and a brother d. infant
Note: Brian had 5 siblings Ronald, Rita, Joan, June, Susan
Barbara Townsend 1939- m 1962 Brian Banks 1938-99
Ann Townsend 1941- m John Keenan d 2015
Andrew Banks 1964- m Sam 1965-
Joanne Banks 1967- m 2003 Alexander Burn 1968
Alexander Banks 1974- Paige Clifford
Jane Keenan 1967- m Mark Cockburn
Matthew Keenan 1969- m Michelle Farrugia
Vicky Keenan 1975- m Richard Green
Charlie 1995- Bella 1993-
Alfie 2002- Ben 2004- Olivia 2007-
Jamie 2008-
Emily Lucy Oliver Tom
Stephanie Louise
Leo Travis
Note: Travis is son by a prior relationship of RG
BANKS

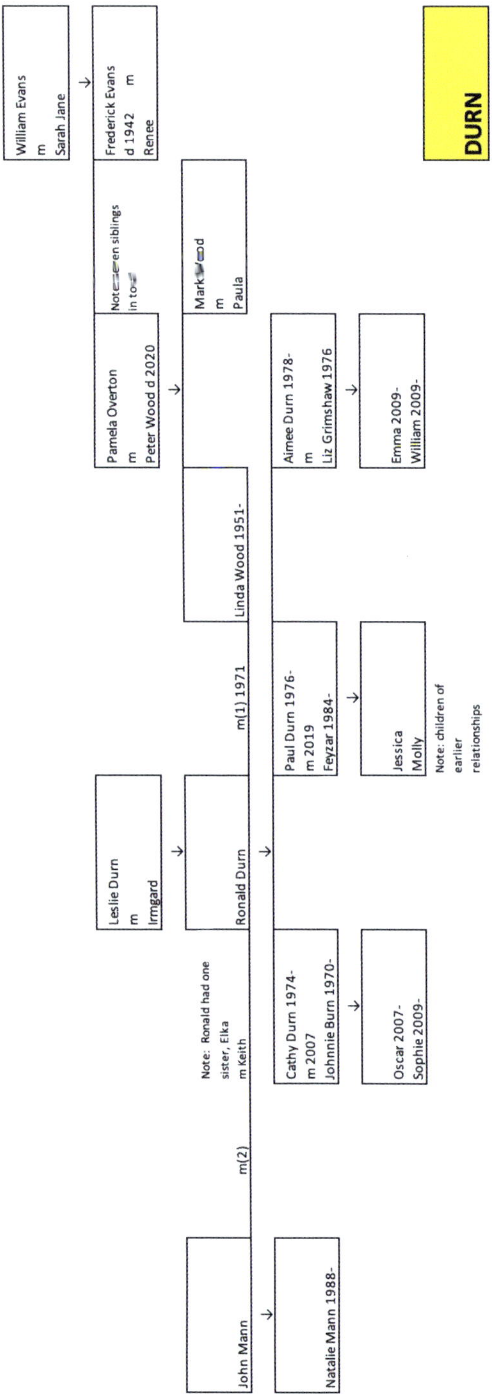
DURN
William Evans m Sarah Jane
Frederick Evans d 1942 m Renee
Note: siblings in to
Mark od m Paula
Pamela Overton m Peter Wood d 2020
Linda Wood 1951-
m(1) 1971
Leslie Durn m Irmgard
Ronald Durn
Note: Ronald had one sister, Elka m Keith
m(2)
John Mann
Natalie Mann 1988-
Cathy Durn 1974- m 2007 Johnnie Burn 1970-
Oscar 2007- Sophie 2009-
Paul Durn 1976- m 2019 Feyzar 1984-
Jessica Molly
Note: children of earlier relationships
Aimee Durn 1978- m Liz Grimshaw 1976
Emma 2009- William 2009-

ENVOI

You may forget, but let me tell you this:

Someone, in some future time, will think of us (Sappho, 600 BC)

Well, my favourite Greek, lady, lyric poet got that right, because I've thought of her quite a bit recently. The sheer chance by which we know her work at all is a miracle – much that we have was found because it was written on papyri used as wrapping paper for Egyptian mummies.

The strange randomness of such a discovery chimes with the randomness of procreation that created the Burn family, any family and indeed the randomness of all creation. And that includes the creation of this book.

Randomness is a plant with unlikely fruit. One day in the far or near future (who knows?) a Burn may achieve greatness or even have greatness thrust upon them, to such a marked degree that people will ask: who is this person, and where did they come from?

Then, they might find this little book and think of us.

ACKNOWLEDGEMENTS

The more I wrote about the slings and arrows of outrageous fortune, I realised that I was repeatedly shooting myself in the foot (and mangling metaphors too). The project was evolving from a chronicle of wasted time into an Orwellian self-denunciation, because the bulk of the events I recounted are descriptions of my own bad behaviour and moral turpitude. There's no escaping this uncomfortable truth. Again, I comfort myself that few will read beyond page one. And besides, the experience has been therapeutic for me.

My thanks to all who provided material and information: Jock Asbury-Bailey, Karen Barnard, Andrew Brand, Janette Bunn, Martin Haddon, Tony Lugg, Robin Ollington, Chrissie Reid, Charlotte Stirling, Caroline Thompson, and Vanessa Whigham. Thanks also to Alex, Annabel and Johnnie, my weirdly tolerant children, for encouragement, suggestions and editorial input.

Finally, to Margie, my muse, my confidante and comforter, my burr under the saddle that made the ride so exciting - thank you

Printed in Great Britain
by Amazon

58510296R00152